1/2 3

D0833674

LAKE COUNTY, ILLINOIS

Pictorial Research by Roxann Marshburn

"Partners in Progress" by Edward Hawley

Produced in cooperation with the
Waukegan/Lake County
Chamber of Commerce

Windsor Publications, Inc.
Northridge, California

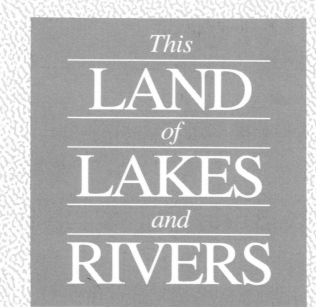

This
LAND
of
LAKES
and
RIVERS

An Illustrated History

by

VIRGINIA MULLERY

Windsor Publications, Inc.—History Books Division
Managing Editor: Karen Story
Design Director: Alexander D'Anca

Staff for *Lake County, Illinois: This Land of Lakes
  and Rivers*

Manuscript Editor: Doreen Nakakihara
Photo Editor: William A. Matthews
Senior Editor, Corporate Biographies: Judith L. Hunter
Production Editor, Corporate Biographies: Phyllis Gray
Senior Proofreader: Susan J. Muhler
Editorial Assistants: Didier Beauvoir, Thelma Fleis-
  cher, Kim Kievman, Rebecca Kropp, Michael
  Nugwynne, Kathy B. Peyser, Pat Pittman,
  Theresa J. Solis
Publisher's Representatives, Corporate Biographies:
  Ken Fiebig and Sandee Frank
Designer: Tanya Maiboroda
Layout Artist: Susan L. Wells

Library of Congress Cataloging-in-Publication Data

Mullery, Virginia, 1928-
    Lake County, Illinois: this land of lakes and rivers/
Virginia Mullery. — 1st ed.
        p.160 cm. 22×28
        "Produced in cooperation with the Waukegan/
Lake County Chamber of Commerce."
        Bibliography: p. 154
        Includes index.
        ISBN 0-89781-267-0
        1. Lake County (Ill.)—History.   2. Lake County
        (Ill.)—Description and travel—Views.   3. Lake
        County (Ill.)—Industries.
        I. Title.
        F547.LM85 1989   88-29194
        977.3'21—dc19   CIP

©1989 Windsor Publications, Inc.
All rights reserved
Published 1989
Printed in the United States of America

Frontispiece: *A clear winter day showcases Lake County's beauty and historical heritage at the replica of Hiram Buttrick's sawmill on Sequoit creek. Photo by Thomas Delany, Jr.*

Right: *Music at the early Lake County fairs was provided by the Libertyville village band, a group of about two dozen musicians. Courtesy, Libertyville-Mundelein Historical Society*

Windsor Publications, Inc.
Elliot Martin, Chairman of the Board
James L. Fish III, Chief Operating Officer
Michele Sylvestro, Vice President/Sales-Marketing

CONTENTS

I dedicate this book to my husband, John Mullery, who "walked" every word of the journey with me,

and

to our children—Mary Alice, Margaret Ann, Catherine, Edward, and Patrick—who represent the future of Lake County. They form a continuity with their father's family, the Mullerys and the Rudds, who were guardians of Lake County's land, and my family, the Flemings and the Lyonses, who were builders of its cities.

Ice dots the Lake Michigan shoreline during the winter. In the distance is the light house at Waukegan Harbor. Photo by Mary Carmody

"When an American says he loves his country, he means not only that he loves the . . . hills, the prairies glistening in the sun or the wide rising plains, the mountains and the seas. He means that he loves an inner air, an inner light in which freedom lives and in which a man can draw the breath of self-respect."

—Adlai Stevenson
Stevenson Sampler

PREFACE

With a county this rich and diverse it is impossible to record every name and event that shaped its history. It is my hope that each reader will weave into the narrative his or her own names and remembrances, thus making it uniquely theirs. For it is as Adlai Stevenson once said, "Everyone has something to contribute to the welfare of his fellow man. No one is unimportant."

Right: Arthur Sheldon ran a business school in present-day Mundelein that was rather ahead of its time, offering employment for women. His motto, "Ability, Reliability, Endurance, and Action" (AREA) gave the town its fourth name (previously it had been Mechanics Grove, Holcomb, and Rockefeller). Sheldon's school eventually went bankrupt and the land he owned in Area was purchased by Cardinal George Mundelein, who gave the village its present name. Courtesy, Libertyville-Mundelein Historical Society

ACKNOWLEDGMENTS

I would like to offer special thanks to the following people who aided and abetted my research: the reference librarians of the Waukegan Public Library, especially Joan Wilts, Marlene Graham, and Sandy Carnelli; Janet Gallimore-Smith and Stacey Pyne Breen of the Lake County Museum; Eloise Daydiff of the Waukegan Historical Society; many staff members of *The News-Sun* but especially Charles Selle, managing editor, who gave me permission to use the files, and librarian Barbara Apple, who helped me to use them; Marie Janik of the Libertyville-Mundelein Historical Society; Warren Wood and other members of the Lake County Department of Planning, Zoning and Environmental Quality; ex-Lake County Board members Rolland Sandee and R.G. Holst; former newsmen Del Wright and Ed Nash; and historians Ruth Mogg and Michael Y. Graham. To the many others who answered questions, pointed me in right directions, and lent their support in dozens of ways, I am also deeply indebted.

Right: *Nestled in the trees of the Ryerson Woods Conservation Area in Deerfield is the small log cabin built in 1928 by Edward and Nora Ryerson. The site along the banks of the Des Plaines River is near where two major Indian trails converged to cross the river. The Ryersons subsequently purchased land to the north along the river, owned by descendants of Daniel Wright, the first white settler in Lake County. The land was donated later to the Lake County Forest Preserve District which Ryerson was instrumental in forming. Photo by Thomas Delany, Jr.*

CHAPTER 1

SHIFTING SANDS

Pleasure boats now ride the waves where once the birchbark canoes of the Potawatomi glided swift and silent. Marinas line the shores where long ago, *voyageurs* paddled their craft into deserted coves and stepped ashore to become the first white men in this land.

The history of Lake County has been shaped for centuries by its waterways: by Lake Michigan to the east and the Chain O'Lakes and the Fox River to the west, by the myriad small lakes, and by the great Des Plaines River and streams that course across the land.

But eons ago there were no lakes and rivers, only the land, barren and silent, buried beneath immense sheets of ice. There were four stages to the Pleistocene glacial epoch, or Ice Age, and the last two, the Illinoian and the Wisconsinian, were responsible for the present topography of Lake County. As the last glacier retreated, meltwaters deposited a rich top soil. The drainageways became the rivers. Large, detached blocks of glacier ice—embedded in glacial till and thus forming depressions—became the lakes, ponds, and swamps.

The Volo Bog in the western part of the county is a living museum of the Ice Age. It was a poorly drained lake with steep sides, which provided conditions conducive to the preservation of plant life. Vegetation dating back 6,000 years has been identified. In 1973 Volo Bog came under the jurisdiction of the Illinois Department of Conservation, and was declared a National Natural Landmark by the United States Department of the Interior.

On the heels of the departing ice came the first human inhabitants of the area. Fluted arrowheads of the Paleo-Indians, who were descendants of people who crossed over from Siberia into Alaska, have been found in the Great Lakes region. These hunters ranged across the land, living off plants and the huge animals that still inhabited the area. Some authorities suggest that the prehistoric animals

Right: *Trees shaped by the Indians can still be found in Lake County. The "Indian Trail Trees," bent and twisted as saplings to grow into their unusual forms, marked the paths to Potawatomi hunting grounds and campsites. This tree at Exmoor Country Club in Highland Park was photographed in 1957. Photo by Hazel Avery, Bannockburn Garden Club. Courtesy, Lake County Museum*

did not succumb to the Ice Age but rather to the weapons of man, and were, perhaps, hunted into extinction.

Evidence of increasingly advanced cultures have been found in Illinois dating back to the Woodland Indians. Famous for their burial mounds these people, whose skeletal remains have been as tall as eight feet, are often referred to as the Mound Builders. Having a highly developed society, they cultivated crops, made beautiful pottery, and buried their dead and their possessions in elaborate mounds. These mounds, some as high as 12 feet, have been found throughout Lake County along the Chain and the Des Plaines, scattered around Wauconda, at Half Day, and near the present Illinois Beach State Park. One which is being preserved and maintained as an educational site by the Forest Preserve District is in Van Patten Woods.

By the middle of the seventeenth century the dominant tribe in Illinois was the Iliniwek, or Illinois. They had 60 known villages throughout the state and had settled into a domestic way of life. But the Iroquois began sending war parties into the region, and by 1750 there were only about 2,000 Iliniwek left in the state. By one estimate their number had dwindled to 50 by 1783.

The Potawatomi, whom most identify with Lake County, were relative latecomers to the scene. Originating farther north, they also were attacked by Iroquois war parties and eventually moved into the Green Bay, Wisconsin, area, where they formed an alliance with the French. An Algonquian tribe, they were closely related to the Ottawas and Ojibwa, or Chippewa.

Local legend has treated the Potawatomi kindly, painting them as a gentle, peaceful people. In fact, they were much more complex. They aggressively moved into Illinois in the eighteenth century and quickly became the dominant tribe in the Lake County area. There were Potawatomi with the early French explorers in Illinois. They allied themselves with the British in the War of 1812 and helped massacre troops at Fort Dearborn. They stayed out of the Black Hawk War, but did help the Americans find the old Sauk's hideout.

The Potawatomi generally were an agricultural people who lived for extended periods in established villages, usually along streams, near springs, or in sheltered bays. During the autumn they traditionally broke up into smaller family groups and moved to winter hunting grounds. In Lake County they have been documented in greatest numbers as living in the Wauconda-Lake Zurich area, and along the shoreline north from Waukegan to near the state line.

Some early historians claim that Jean Nicolet, a French trader known to have visited Indian villages along the Fox River in Wisconsin in 1634, ranged as far south as Lake County. However, Louis Jolliet and Father Jacques Marquette are the first white men documented to have visited the area.

Jolliet, a Canadian, was a knowledgeable woodsman, compatible with the Indians, and an expert mapmaker. Marquette was a Jesuit priest from France, committed to evangelizing the "savages." Together they formed a team to go in search of the great river to the south of Sault Sainte Marie. In two 20-foot-long canoes, with Indian guides, they left St. Ignace (Michigan) on May 17, 1673, and about three days later entered the present state of Illinois. They floated down the Mississippi, according to Marquette's journal, as far as the Arkansas River. On the return trip they were persuaded by the Indians to cross the state via the Illinois and Des Plaines rivers, finally traveling north on Lake Michigan. En route they camped along the shoreline and, according to entries in Marquette's journal, he probably celebrated Mass on Christmas on the present Waukegan beach.

The two parted at the DePere (Wisconsin) mission, where Marquette remained due to ill health. Unfortunately, Jolliet's boat capsized on his way home. All of his maps and documents were lost, leaving only Marquette's vague and possibly inaccurate journal to record the explorations. In the fall of 1674 Marquette made a second trip via the Lake Michigan route, to establish a mission at Kaskaskia. He died in 1675 on the trip home.

When the two men first gazed upon Illinois, Jolliet was moved to say of the region, "[This is] the most beautiful and the most easily settled."

Illinois was claimed for France by explorer Rene Robert Cavelier, Sieur de La Salle, who ventured into the area in the 1680s, and it was ruled from Quebec. Following the French and Indian War all of New France, which included Illinois, was ceded to the British by the Treaty of Paris in 1763. Then on July 4, 1778, George Rogers Clark captured Kaskaskia and all of Illinois for the Americans. By the Ordinance of 1787 the Northwest Territory, which included Illinois, was established.

A military government under Arthur St. Clair was formed, and three judges were appointed. The few pioneers in the sparsely settled territory had no voice in choosing their government. In Lake County it was of little importance since the Potawatomi, the only inhabitants, were unconcerned with the white man's government.

By 1798 the territory had reached the magic number of 5,000 male inhabitants, which earned them the right to elect their own representatives. Things moved right along, and Congress created the Territory of Illinois on February 3, 1809. The capitol was at Kaskaskia, and Ninian Edwards was appointed as governor. In the years immediately following, counties were realigned frequently, with the present Lake County falling successively into Clair, Madison, and Crawford counties.

When the time arrived to talk of statehood, Lake County came close to being drawn right off the map of Illinois. The Ordinance of 1787 decreed that the northern boundaries of Indiana and Illinois be drawn through the southern tip of Lake Michigan. But when Indiana was admitted to the Union in 1816 the ordinance was ignored, and its border was drawn 10 miles north.

Using this precedent Nathaniel Pope, Illinois delegate to Congress, asked the same for Illinois, according to Robert P. Howard, author of *Illinois—A History of the Prairie State.* Pope then amended his proposal to place the northern boundary 41 miles north of the southern tip of the lake. He argued: "Illinois is sure to be a great state. Its great extent of territory, its unrivaled fertility of soil, its capacity for sustaining a dense population, together with its commanding position would, in

Below: *A circa 1910 postcard depicts a young woman standing in the "V" formed by another Indian Trail Tree—this one a massive oak tree once situated along Scranton Avenue in Lake Bluff, not far from Sheridan Road. Sheridan was an early Indian trail to the Chicago portage. Courtesy, Lake County Museum*

Snow scenes along the frozen Des Plaines River remind one that Lake County is subject to all the vagaries of a Chicago winter, with arctic temperatures that reach as far below as minus 26 degrees, and accompanied by wind chill factors down to 60 degrees below zero. Photo by Mary Carmody

Above: *The waterways of Lake County have contributed much to its growth both in industrial and recreational activities. Photo by Thomas Delany, Jr.*

Left: *This is an artist's conception of the site of Waukegan as seen by French explorer La Salle and his party in October 1679. The first trading post on Lake Michigan was established here. Courtesy, Lake County Museum*

course of time give the new state a very controlling influence with her sister states . . ."

The amendment passed easily. Wisconsin was still a wilderness, and no one was there to protest.

In another innovative move, Pope offered a second amendment. Precedent had been established for allotting 5 percent of proceeds from sales of public lands to be returned to the states for roads and canals. Pope asked that in Illinois the figures be amended to give 2 percent to Congress for building roads leading to the state and 3 percent to be spent on schools, including a college or university.

The bill granting Illinois statehood was signed into law on April 18, 1818, but its enactment hinged on a population of 40,000. Although hard put to come up with that many people, a questionable census resulted in a figure of just over 40,000.

A state constitution was written and elections were held, and President James Monroe signed the papers to finalize Illinois' statehood on December 3, 1818. News reached the frontier two weeks later and on December 13, inhabitants of the new state—however many there were—celebrated.

Early the following year Clark County was created, which included the present Lake County. Two years later the map was redrawn, and the present Lake County was put into the newly created Pike County. Most of the population of the state was still concentrated in the south, with the population of Pike estimated at 700 to 800.

After another round of map changes Cook County was established in 1831, and in 1835 the Cook County Commissioners Court designated a voting precinct named Lake. Hiram Kennicott was elected as the first justice of the peace on October 17, 1835. The same court appointed Richard Steele, Thomas McClure, and Mark Noble to establish a road from the forks of the Chicago River up the Des Plaines.

The 1830s marked a series of events which turned the eyes of Yankees and newly arriving immigrants west toward Lake County. The Erie Canal, completed in 1825, opened a water route from New York. A rough military road, from Detroit to Chicago along the Green Bay trail, was designated a post road

for stagecoaches. And in 1835 work on the long-discussed and bandied-about Illinois and Michigan Canal, first visualized by Jolliet, began to bring a flood of Irish laborers to the area.

Perhaps more importantly the Indians of northern Illinois led by a Sauk, Black Hawk, had been subdued in what proved to be a last stand. In the fall of 1833 the Indian tribes of northern Illinois and southern Wisconsin were summoned to a council in Chicago to negotiate a treaty and land transfer. More than 5,000 Indians, including the Potawatomi from Lake County, encamped around the village. Unscrupulous entrepreneurs moved in and set up shop as well. Between them and the wild, noisy ceremonies of the Indians, the whole affair took on the appearance of a carnival. Finally, an agreement was hammered out in which the Indians ceded the last large remaining block of land in the old Northwest Territory: from Chicago north to the Milwaukee River. One of the old chiefs at the meeting was Aptegtizhek, for whom the town of Aptakisic is named. (It means Half Day, the name of another area town.) But the chief negotiators for the Indians were Shabbonee, an Ottawa; Alexander Robinson, who was Ottawa and British; and Billy Caldwell, of Mohawk and Irish ancestry.

In return for some 500 million acres of land, the Potawatomi received $100,000 cash and $100,000 in goods, various annuities, a promise to pay debts incurred during the encampment, and lands in Kansas and Missouri, where they promised to relocate no later than September 1836. Although the treaty was not ratified until 1835, most were soon gone. Always a migratory people, some chose their own destination and moved to Canada, where their descendants continue to live on islands in Lake Huron. Other Potawatomi can be found today on the Prairie Band Reserve near Topeka, Kansas.

The Indians left behind a virgin wilderness, scarcely touched by their presence. The settlers following in their wake, along three main routes from Chicago, found an unparalleled panorama of nature's opulence in Lake County.

Those coming north along the shore of Lake Michigan followed the long, sweeping

Facing page, bottom: *This log church, St. Mary of the Woods Chapel, originally stood at Lincoln Avenue and Green Bay Road in Highland Park. In the 1850s it was moved several miles north, where it also served as a schoolhouse. One of the earliest Catholic churches in the county, it was served by a circuit priest. The large walnut cross was erected in August 1853. Courtesy, Lake County Museum*

curve of the lake, from which rose abrupt clay-cliff walls cut through by wooded ravines. At the southern reaches of what became Waukegan the bluffs flattened out into a kind of terrace, which came to be called the Waukegan flats. From Waukegan north to the state line, the landscape changed to the sand dunes which—still in their pristine beauty—make up the Illinois Beach State Park. Dune grasses, rushes, and sedges marked the sandy areas. Willows and lindens could be found at the foot of the bluffs. The flats were covered with a profusion of wildflowers and plants such as trailing juniper and bearberry, with its thick, evergreen leaves and tiny, pale-pink, bell-shaped blossoms. White pines also were abundant in the area.

Timber lands lay to the east of the Des Plaines River, along which other early settlers moved. To the west, at the southern end, prairies stretched to the horizon, while at the northern end were many stands of oak and hickory. Tall, golden prairie grass interspersed with equally tall flowers created a palette of colors in one place, and an undergrowth of hawthorn, wild crab, and sumac in another gave the county a wildly beautiful and variegated landscape.

Other settlers moved in along the fingers of the North Branch, called the Skokies. The land around these waterways was always marshy: never wooded, but covered with indigenous marsh grasses and reeds.

Yet others followed a fourth, less heavily traveled route into the Fox River Valley—which also changed its face from forests of oak in the southwestern corner to marshes in the north.

Captain Daniel Wright, a veteran of the War of 1812, and his wife, Ruth Todd Wright,

were the first white couple to put down roots in Lake County. Their journey began in New England, where Wright had been born in 1778. They moved to Ohio, where they lived for 20 years before Wright again looked west. He traveled to Chicago, where he paused briefly before pushing further north along the North Branch to the Indian village of Half Day. Wright arrived in June 1834, and with the help of the Indians immediately built a 20-by-20-foot cabin on what is now Milwaukee Avenue between Deerfield and Aptakisic roads. That completed, he sent for his wife. She traveled from Ohio with their seven children, two oxen, and one cow. It is interesting to note that Wright was 56 years old when he came to this area, quite an advanced age in those times.

Life in the wilderness was seldom idyllic. In the first fall, a prairie fire destroyed Wright's winter hay. Then a young son took sick and died, and three days later Ruth Wright, too, was dead. In the fall of 1835 one of Wright's grown sons died. Far from doctors, with no close place to replenish goods and isolated by miles of wilderness, there was little to rely on but their ingenuity, strong backs, and tough determination. It is a wonder that these intrepid men and women hung on and kept coming, and finally laid the foundation for the Lake County of today.

Despite the rigors Wright—who had married a second time—lived to the age of 95. He died on December 30, 1873. His daughter, Caroline, married a new neighbor, William Wigham, in January 1836. The ceremony was the first in Lake County and was performed by Justice Hiram Kennicott. Also a neighbor, Kennicott had studied law under Millard Fillmore, the 13th president of the United States. It was not until several years later that the Reverend Samuel Hurlbut, a Methodist, arrived in the area and, according to a historian, "broke the monopoly of the justices in marriage fees."

After McHenry County, which included Lake, was set off from Cook, it was reported that no probate business had been done at McHenry during the years of 1837 to 1839. "The settlers were few and were for the most part young and vigorous. They seemed to be more intent on marriage than on departing this

Above: *Captain Daniel Wright, Lake County's first white settler, was 56 years old when he arrived in Half Day in June 1834. With the assistance of nearby Indians led by Chief Mettawa, he built a 20-by-20-foot cabin near the Des Plaines River. He was joined by his wife, Ruth, and seven children in August, but his wife and youngest son died shortly after their arrival. Wright himself lived to be 95 years old and is buried in Half Day Cemetery. Courtesy, E.W. Plonien Collection, Waukegan Historical Society*

Above: An early settler's cabin northeast of Libertyville is believed to have belonged to the Stolzman family. The original Vardin's cabin, the first in "Vardin's Grove" (now Libertyville), was recreated for the town's Sesquicentennial celebration in 1987. The cabin is located in Cook Park, near its original site, and was used as Libertyville's first post office. Courtesy, Waukegan Historical Society

world," historian John Halsey commented.

Close on the Wrights' heels, settlers began to move up the Des Plaines: brothers Richard and Ransom Steele in 1835 to Libertyville, where the following year Richard's son, Albert, was the first white child born in the county; Leonard and George Gage, who gave their names to a lake in 1835; and Amos Bennett, a black who often was referred to as "Dr. Bennett" for his healing skill with herbs and who once called himself the "first white man [non-Indian] that ever planted corn on the O'Plaine River within Lake County."

The river road they followed ended at the Gurnee ford in Warren Township. It crossed over to higher land at Yorkhouse, where a trail continued up Mill Creek to the state line. Jacob Miller established the first mill in the county on Mill Creek in 1835, but it closed down when he perished on the way to the California Gold Rush of 1849.

Settlement along the lake began higher up, and was more concentrated in Benton and Waukegan townships than in Shields and Deerfield. Nelson Landon and Jeremiah Stowell came up Green Bay Road in 1835 riding one pony, on which they took turns. Traveling almost to the state line, they finally decided that the fine upland prairies of Benton were "good enough." Landon built a cabin and sent for his bride, Phoebe, to join him. It is said she spent two winters on the prairie before she saw another white woman, and that during that time she bore a child.

Landon left a record of some of his purchases during those first years on the frontier. For a barrel of flour he paid $35; for a barrel of pork, $25; and for a bushel of potatoes, $3.50. He served as a county commissioner, and died in 1884.

French maps showed a trading post at Little Fort, which later became Waukegan, early in the eighteenth century. Later excavators claimed to have found timbers on the bluff above the lake which dated to that early post. In 1835 Thomas Jenkins arrived on the scene, and by 1836 he had built and stocked a two-story frame store just below the site of the French post. Soon tiring of the wilderness, he returned to Chicago. A second storekeeper, James Gorton, tried to open on the spot—but a dispute about occupancy forced him to set up shop further west at the "O'Plaine Bridge."

It would be difficult to blame Jenkins for leaving. An eyewitness account in 1837 reported only three small log huts in Little Fort—two below the bluff and one in the trees on the flats, which were "so thick you couldn't see the lake."

But the harbor was excellent, the land on the bluff was high and dry, and the farm lands to the west were rich. Soon all roads led to Little Fort, as the port of shipment and entry. The fledgling community grew, attracting doctors, lawyers, merchants, and chiefs.

Land around Little Fort began to be claimed by people like Peleg Sunderlin, who ran a tavern and stage stop on Green Bay Road; Thomas Tiernan, who staked out a farm where the Belvidere Mall now stands; John Mullery, at Five Points in what is now North Chicago; John and Catherine Kloes (later spelled Cloes) in present Lake Bluff; Michael Dulanty in West Lake Forest; and William and Mary Dwyer, who ran an influential stage stop on Green Bay Road. These people, and dozens more like them, came from 1835 to 1839.

A fourth area of settlement in the county was in the Fox Valley, on the western fringes. Lake Zurich and Ela were on what was called "the great highway," between Chicago and McHenry. George Ela, who settled there in 1835, later became a member of the Illinois legislature. Charles Fletcher arrived in Fremont Township the same year, having walked all the way from Buffalo, New York.

The settlement of Antioch and Grant townships began somewhat later, since tillable land was limited by the abundance of lakes and marshland. But late in 1836, Darius and Thomas Gage and Thomas Warner came to the region to stake a claim. Returning to Chicago by a different route than the one by which they had arrived, they lost their way in a December storm and nearly perished. Fortunately they stumbled onto the home of Willard Jones in Warren Township, and lived to become the first settlers in Antioch.

Eyewitness accounts of those days remain. Judge E.S. Ingalls recalled arriving as a boy with his family in the spring of 1838 and building a cabin in a grove of burr oak, one mile north of Spring Grove on Nippersink Creek. They soon discovered that although settlers lived 10 to 20 miles apart, some early English settlers in the area desired to keep the entire region open for their late-arriving friends and neighbors. Americans moving into the area protested, and the contest was heating up. Not wanting to be part of the feud, the Ingallses moved to Antioch.

There, Ingalls remembered, Indians came down from Wisconsin in the fall and winter to fish and trap in the "Pistakee Lakes," and often continued on to trap raccoon in the Little Fort river. "That's the only way we knew such a place existed," Ingalls recalled.

John Salisbury, who arrived in Chicago with five cents, left behind a picture of his first log cabin near Fox Lake. It was one room, 7 by 9 feet, with a fireplace in one corner, a table in another, a workbench in the third, and the entrance in the fourth. The family's six children slept in a loft.

With the influx of settlers it soon became apparent that rules governing the acquisition of land were needed, in order to prevent land grabs by the greedy or speculative. At a meeting in Independence Grove (now Libertyville) on December 2, 1836, residents voted on a code of resolutions and regulations called The Compact. Governed by an elected commission, it remained the voice of authority in the area until the Illinois State Legislature passed laws to protect property rights in the burgeoning county.

McHenry County, which included Lake, had been set off from Cook County earlier that year, and in March 1837 it was determined that the new county had the 350 white inhabitants necessary to allow the organization to become effective. In June 1837 an election was held, with the majority of those registered living east of the Fox River.

The new government promptly levied a one percent property tax on "slaves, pleasure carriages, distillery, stock in trade, livestock, lumber, clocks, and watches." This was curious, since slavery was not an issue in northern Illinois nor with most of the Yankees who settled the area. It can only be surmised that they borrowed the wording for their document from one in effect in the South. It is also interesting to note that land was not taxed.

Roads began to be surveyed, and every man between the ages of 21 and 50 was required to work on the roads for five days a year or pay 75 cents a day.

Stage stops or taverns on the frontier often were gathering places for local residents, providing these people who for the most part lived in great isolation with a place to socialize and enjoy lively conversation. One of the most influential, from the standpoint of politics, was the establishment on Green Bay Road near Lake Bluff operated by Irish immigrants William and Mary Dwyer. Dr. Richard Murphy, Mary Dwyer's brother, lived with them. Political activists before they arrived in the Midwest, the three soon became embroiled in local politics. The tavern was the setting for debate, civic meetings, and endorsement of causes and candidates.

When the newly elected McHenry County commissioners divided it into precincts and magistrate districts, they appointed William Dwyer supervisor of Oak District and Richard Murphy justice of Oak Magistrate District. Murphy soon moved up the political ladder, and was elected to the state legislature in 1838. Serving three terms, he was responsible for drafting and pushing into enactment the Illinois Public School Law.

Public sentiment began to build for splitting Lake and McHenry counties. Murphy, who had run on a plank favoring division, was instrumental in finally pushing it through the Illinois Assembly on March 1, 1839. As of that date Lake County, as it exists geographically today, was born.

Right: *Roosevelt Park's scenic ravines offered up more of Waukegan's healthful mineral waters. The "Quintette Springs," a series of five springs, were owned by Judge W.K. McAllister, a state supreme court judge in the early 1870s. Each of the five springs was said to cure a different disease. The park is located at the southwest corner of Belvidere Street and McAlister Avenue. Courtesy, E.W. Plonien Collection, Waukegan Historical Society*

CHAPTER 2

ANCHORED
TO THE
LAND

Scarcely had the candles been blown out on the birthday cake, than the celebrants were at odds with one another.

Libertyville, centrally located in the county, was an up-and-coming settlement on a main road between Chicago and Milwaukee. Started when George Vardin settled beside a grove halfway between Butler's Lake and the Des Plaines River in 1835, it became known as Vardin's Grove. But Vardin left, and when a group of farm families gathered to celebrate the Fourth of July the following year, they decided to rename their settlement Independence Grove. However, when the establishment of a post office soon after led to the discovery that there was already an Independence Grove in the state, the settlement was given its third name: Libertyville.

Little Fort, on the other hand, was developing more slowly despite its potential as a port city. The three commissioners from Cook County appointed by the legislature to select the new county seat quickly chose Libertyville.

Little Fort proponents bided their time, and concentrated on the upcoming election of county commissioners. They succeeded in getting one of their men, Nelson Landon, into office. The other two elected, Charles Bartlett and Jared Gage, favored Libertyville.

The three men met for the first time on August 17, 1839, and Landon adroitly convinced the other two that due to their lack of funds, they should put off erecting a building and temporarily rent quarters.

Richard Murphy was returned to the legislature as the representative from Lake County. He favored Little Fort for the county seat, and in 1840 was influential in the taking of the national census. The state census taker in Lake County, Captain Morris Robinson,

Right: *Approaching the shore of Little Fort in May 1847, artist R.N. White portrayed a busy community of 1,237 people with an active harbor trade. The D.O. Dickinson warehouse is prominent at the base of the pier, at the foot of Water Street. Dickinson, who also operated a gristmill, was the first president of the Village of Little Fort, incorporated April 13, 1849, with a population of 2,500. Courtesy, Waukegan Historical Society*

Below: *The location of the county seat caused heated controversy between Libertyville and Little Fort. Accusations of impropriety plagued the election but Little Fort won out, and the first courthouse, right, was erected in 1841 at County, Madison, and Utica streets. To the left is the Lake County Recorder office building. Photo by E.W. Plonien. Courtesy, Lake County Museum*

went about his appointed duties with a message for everyone he talked to: the advantage of Little Fort as county seat. Securing petitions along with head counts, he walked to the state capitol in order to deliver them before the close of the session.

On February 17, 1841, the legislature called for an election to be held on April 5 regarding the location of the county seat. Accusations of improprieties flew. For example, the *Little Fort Porcupine and Democratic Banner*, rehashing the controversial election several years later, stated, "The census showed 720 males over 20, yet 744 votes were cast."

Nevertheless, the ballots were taken at face value—with 278 cast for Libertyville and 466 for Little Fort. On April 13, the county seat was formally relocated.

This time Landon moved quickly to construct a building that would anchor the county seat to Little Fort. In order to do this the commissioners borrowed $200 from Elmsley Sunderlin, and on April 20—just 15 days after the election—the sale of land was recorded in Chicago. A court house was contracted for $3,800 and a jail for $1,000.

Archimedes Wynkoop, publisher of the *Little Fort Porcupine*, also was the county recorder, the deputy clerk, and a hard loser. He moved his office back to Libertyville and the clerk, Henry B. Steele, satisfied that Wynkoop was doing all the work, said nary a word.

At the instigation of Landon, the commissioners voted to discharge Steele as negli-

gent and incompetent because he was not serving his office personally. They fined Wynkoop $10. Petulantly, he would not turn over the seal at once, forcing the commissioners to have a new one made.

Harassed by debts, Wynkoop went to the Gold Rush in 1849, leaving his wife and children behind. Forty years later he died in California, according to Halsey. What became of his wife and children is not recorded.

Meanwhile, Steele was in a revolving door. It was determined that Landon had not been properly sworn into office when he called the meeting to oust Steele, so the circuit court ordered Steele back into office. In January 1843 the state legislature voted to declare the acts of the commissioners legal and binding, and Steele was out again.

Murphy, a force to be reckoned with in the legislature, worked for the passage of the act which ordained that the county seat of Lake County "hereby permanently be situated at Little Fort." Chairman of the powerful house committee on banks and corporations, Murphy also fought to change the apportionment law so that state senators could be elected from Lake County as well as Cook. He has been described by Halsey as "well equipped to take his place in the hurly-burly of prairie politics where duels and intrigue were not uncommon."

According to Halsey, Murphy had no superior in this part of the country and was described as a polished gentleman, forceful speaker, and popular physician. Nevertheless, after losing a hotly contested election bordering on the vindictive to Libertyville pioneer Horace Butler in 1844, Murphy never ran for office again.

Little Fort numbered 150 souls in 1844. Shipments arriving in the harbor amounted to 202 tons, and 64,000 bushels of wheat were shipped out. Previously all roads had led to

Chicago, which was considered the market town. But it took three to four days to transport a load of hay to Chicago, in contrast to the day's journey to Little Fort.

In just two years the population had increased fivefold. Incoming merchandise had tripled in volume as had the wheat being shipped from Little Fort—184,000 bushels. One of the leading merchants was D.O. Dickinson, who operated a gristmill and warehouse. His was the first name that ships coming into the harbor saw, prominently displayed on the long pier which he had built at the foot of Water Street.

There was money to be made in the new towns, and it was easy for men to rise quickly to places of prominence. Dickinson grew up in a family of limited circumstances in Ellisburg, New York, and arrived in Little Fort in 1841. Within two years he was elected treasurer and assessor of Lake County, and in August 1843 was host to a group of men and women who organized the First Congregational Church of Little Fort.

Dickinson's warehouse was often the setting for political gatherings, and court was held there while the courthouse was being built. When Little Fort's population reached the 2,500 mark, it was incorporated as a village. The date was April 13, 1849, and Dickinson was elected the first president.

Earlier that year, the name of the village had been changed to Waukegan, the Potawatomi equivalent of "fort" or "trading post." A "ce" on the end of the word would have indicated "little," and that was exactly what the residents of the burgeoning town did not want.

The new courthouse was a fine structure. There also were more than 60 other commercial buildings in town and a number of industries, including a flour mill and brickyards. While the town grew the world continued to shrink, as a newly installed telegraph line linked Waukegan and other communities to the major cities.

News could now reach the prairies faster and more accurately, and newspapers continued to play a critical role in people's lives. Those pioneer editors and publishers were usually the sole source of national and state news in their communities, and lent their colorful commentary.

The *Porcupine,* Lake County's first newspaper, was published from 1845 to 1847. There were a number of short-lived papers in those early years, but the next one of note was the *Chronicle,* which began to be published in 1847. The *Chronicle* was bought in 1855 and its name was changed to the *Chronicle/Advocate.* With its name changed again, to the *Independent Democrat,* it discontinued publication in 1857.

The first issue of the *Waukegan Weekly Gazette* hit the street on October 12, 1850. It announced that it was Whig in politics, and supported harbor improvement, distribution of public lands, and free schools. Although its offices were destroyed by fire in 1856, the paper continued to be published for 61 years until it was absorbed by the *Daily Sun.*

Early in 1845, the editor of the *Porcupine* bemoaned the fact that the town contained "seven places where liquor is sold by the small and two in the quantity, and yet we have not even one church."

It is true that church buildings did not exist, but the Congregationalists had been organized since 1843. After meeting for the first time in the home of D.O. and Susan Dickinson, the Reverend C.C. Cadwell was asked to be pastor. Services continued to be held in the homes of members. A church was dedicated

Below: *It was 15 years after the original courthouse was destroyed by fire in 1875 when these employees posed at the entrance of the new building. In back, from left, are: George Hutchison; James Jamesion; A.L. Hendee, the county clerk; and Andrew Conrad. In front are Louis Dorsett, Judge Francis Clark, Ada Kinnie, and Jennie Thomas. Photo by E.W. Plonien. Courtesy, Lake County Museum*

Above: *The Little Fort Baptist Church, organized in 1845, held its first baptisms in the Little Fort river. Located next door on Genesee Street is the Waukegan Academy (site of the present-day Academy Theater), built in 1848. Isaac Clarke was the first principal of the private school, which offered English, Greek, Latin, German, French, Spanish, science, mathematics, music, and philosophy. Tuition was $2 to $5.25 per course, with lab courses an extra 50 cents. In 1853 enrollment was 250, including 80 women. Courtesy, E.W. Plonien Collectin, Waukegan Historical Society*

Right: *Organized in 1843, the First Congregational Church of Waukegan completed this building in 1862 at the corner of Utica Street and Grand Avenue. The building was destroyed by fire in 1940. The Reverend C.C. Cadwell was asked to be pastor of the original congregation, which first met in the members' homes. Courtesy, E.W. Plonien Collection, Waukegan Historical Society*

on September 14, 1845, according to church records, but no indication of its location remains. Selling that church to another congregation several years later, they built a second time on the site of the present First Presbyterian Church. But when the Presbyterians with whom they had worshiped separated from them in 1857, the Congregationalists were once again without a church. Finally in 1862 they built at the corner of Utica Street and Grand Avenue, on the site of their present church.

A year after the Congregationalists formed, the first Catholic parish in the county, St. Bernard (later renamed Immaculate Conception), was established in Little Fort on two lots at the corner of Water and Utica streets. The lots were sold to the diocese by Michael Dulanty, whose public house occupied the adjoining lot. This church, completed in 1847, grew out of the mission efforts of Father John Gueguen, a circuit riding priest. He said Mass from Rockford to Mendota, stopping regularly in Little Fort, at Dwyer's settlement in Lake Bluff, and on Michael Yore's land in west Lake Forest in a building known as the Corduroy Church.

Lake County is known to have been on the Methodist circuit riding district as well in the 1830s, with evidence that the Reverend Washington Wilcox held services in Half Day, at York House, on Corduroy Road, and in Lake Bluff on the shoreline.

At the invitation of John and Elizabeth Strong, who farmed at Five Points in what is now North Chicago, the Reverend Isaac W. Hallam came to Little Fort during a February snowstorm in 1845 to conduct Episcopal services at the Exchange Hotel and baptize the Strongs' baby. Monthly services started soon after and Christ parish was organized a year later, with early services held in the courthouse.

The Baptists also were organized in Little Fort in 1845, and the first baptisms were held in the Little Fort River.

Sixteen Congregationalists living in the vicinity of Ivanhoe earned the distinction of organizing the first church in the county. Mercy Payne, a widow who had sold her farm in New York and traveled west with her sons and their families, called the first meeting in her log cabin home at the corner of the present Route 176 and Midlothian Road on April 20, 1838. They were organized as Presbyterian, by virtue of an agreement between the Presbyterian and Congregational denominations that all frontier churches in the Northwest Territory be Presbyterian-governed by a joint board. The Reverend John Blatchford was called to serve the church, which was known as Mechanics Grove (Mundelein) Presbyterian Church. Members traveled by ox cart to one another's cabins for services until 1845, when a church was built in Libertyville. Returning eventually to Ivanhoe, the original founders reverted to their Congregationalist roots and in 1856 finally built the church that still stands today.

In 1849, the same year that Little Fort changed its name, the county voted to adopt

the township form of government—an option granted by the state legislature. In Lake County, where so many voters had New England roots, there was no contest between the town form of government and the Southern system of commissioners. Townships won: 1,692 votes to 3.

Josiah Moulton of Benton, Michael Dulanty of Waukegan, and Elijah Haines of Avon and Waukegan were appointed to divide the county and name the new townships. Haines, who was master of the first school in Little Fort in 1841 and who later served in the Illinois legislature, recorded much of the early history of the county in *Historical and Statistical Sketches of Lake County,* published in 1852.

Benton Township was named for Thomas Hart Benton, a popular United States senator from Missouri who championed the rights of the common man and advocated free public lands for settlers.

Newport was the name chosen by the people, receiving 70 votes to Mortimer's 7 and Verona's 2.

Avon was a compromise name chosen over Eureka and Hainesville, whose petitioners had reached a stalemate. Hainesville, which had a population of 200 and in 1846 had earned the distinction of being the first village to be incorporated in the county, had seemed a logical choice. No record remains of who proposed Avon, but being the name of a river in England, it has been suggested that it appealed to settlers with English roots.

Antioch was chosen because of its biblical connotations, courtesy of a large group of settlers who belonged to a religious sect called

the Disciples.

Warren got its name from Warren, New York—the former home of two settlers, Amos Wright and Alex Druse.

Grant was first named Goodale for Deveraux Goodale, who promised to donate money for a town house. But he reneged, and in 1867 the name was changed to Grant in honor of the Civil War general. Ironically, it has been noted that Grant was the only township that did not give Ulysses S. Grant a majority when he ran for president in 1868.

Shields was named for James Shields, a United States senator and a veteran of the Mexican War; Fremont in honor of John Charles Fremont, a general and an explorer; and Ela for George Ela, a pioneer leader.

George Washington's home on the Potomac lent its name to Vernon Township, while Wauconda was adopted from the Indian word meaning "spirit waters."

Cuba, first dubbed Troy until it was learned that name was already taken, owes its name to the popular interest in the island generated by President James Polk's offer to buy it from Spain.

Residents of Deerfield voted with the following results: Erin, 13; Deerfield, 17. Libertyville and Waukegan obviously took the names of their principal towns.

Waukegan's star was rising, and funds for an expansion of the harbor were sought. It was reported that often during 1854, although three long, wooden piers extended out onto the lake, as many as 300 teams would have to stand in line and wait to unload grain onto ships. Most of them probably came in from the west on the new Plank Road (now Belvidere Road, or Route 120), completed just a year or two earlier to the tune of $2,000 a mile.

In 1847 Congress appropriated funds for a lighthouse to be built below the bluff, and in 1852 another $15,000 was designated for the building of a harbor—but when the money ran out, the work was halted. In 1856 sympathizers tried to get Congress to release an additional $35,000 but after much debate, including questions on the location of Waukegan (lawmakers had never heard of it), the bill was defeated, 17 to 16. Perhaps the plans were too grand speculated E.P. DeWolf, writing in John Halsey's *A History of Lake County, Illi-*

Above: *Schoolmaster, surveyor, town planner, justice of the peace, lawyer, legislator, researcher, historian, newspaper founder—Elijah M. Haines surely left a legacy in Lake County. The county's first incorporated town, Hainesville, still bears his name, and two lengthy books he wrote and a third he edited record much of Lake County's early history. On his death in 1889, at age 67, almost the entire state general assembly attended his funeral. Courtesy, Lake County Museum Collection, Waukegan Historical Society*

Left: *The first service of Christ Church parish was held in Cory's Exchange Hotel to baptize the infant son of North Chicago farmers John and Elizabeth Strong. The courthouse became the home of the Episcopalian congregation for four years until 1850, when the "little brick church" at Grand Avenue and Utica Street in Waukegan was begun. This 1867 photo shows the stained-glass Rose Window (partially hidden by trees) that is incorporated into the present brownstone Romanesque and Gothic church, dedicated in 1889 and still in use today. Photo by R.W. Hook. Courtesy, Waukegan Historical Society*

Facing page, top: The Ansel B. Cook home, built in 1876 on the site of the first permanent dwelling in Libertyville, today houses the Libertyville-Mundelein Historical Society. The Victorian framehouse, distinguished by its seven chimneys, has been restored. Cook, a state legislator from Cook County and later president of the Chicago City Council, is better known for his work as a stonemason, having done the masonry work on Chicago's famous Water Tower, along with a number of buildings redone after the Chicago Fire and still in use today. Courtesy, Libertyville-Mundelein Historical Society

Below: The Ivanhoe Congregational Church celebrated its sesquicentennial in 1988. Founded in 1838 by a group of 16 Congregationalists living near the Ivanhoe-Libertyville-Mundelein area, the church members held services in various nearby communities until 1856, when it built the church that still stands. Courtesy, Waukegan News-Sun

nois. Or more likely, the Illinois representatives in Congress all were from Chicago and little concerned about Lake County.

When the first train came chugging into Waukegan on New Year's Day in 1855, the economic future of the town seemed assured. The Illinois Parallel Railroad Company, chartered on February 17, 1851, soon changed its name to the Chicago and Milwaukee Railroad. It was to meet the Milwaukee and Chicago Railroad at the state line.

The first regular train carrying dignitaries from Chicago arrived on January 11, to the celebratory sounds of pealing church bells, band music, and a cannon round. Waukegan village board officials greeted the visitors, and dinner for 400 people followed in Dickinson's Hall. (The hall was on the second floor of a store building erected by Dickinson on the bluff about 1850, according to the *Historical Encyclopedia of Illinois*.) The *Gazette* reported that "Newark Cider, commonly called champagne" was served, which the editor found regrettable. Many Chicagoans stayed over for a grand ball that evening.

Early timetables announced one train a day from Chicago and one returning from Waukegan, with the trip taking two hours each way. Before the Milwaukee link was completed in May 1855, stages met the trains at Waukegan and carried northbound passengers to Kenosha, Racine, or Milwaukee.

Henry Blodgett was the attorney for the railroad, and was instrumental in pushing the single-track rail lines to completion. In 1866 the railroad was leased to the Chicago and North Western Railroad.

According to Elmer Vliet's history of Lake Bluff, Walter S. Gurnee—president of the Chicago and Milwaukee Railroad—speculated on the fact that Chicago was filling up with refugees from the potato famine in Ireland and civil strife in Germany. He shrewdly foresaw that the well-to-do would want to escape the city and its growing pains to a more tranquil life in Lake County. He acquired land all along the new railroad, and at Port Clinton—which consisted of a sawmill, a few stores, and a pier—his Port Clinton Land Company subdivided over 1,000 acres. He hung a sign at the depot reading "Highland Park," which he considered a more enticing name. Gurnee sold the land to a developer when he moved back East, and the city of Highland Park was incorporated in 1867.

Gurnee was right on several counts. Men were making fortunes in Chicago, and there was now time to think of things like higher education. The impetus came from religious groups, with the Methodists leading the way and establishing Northwestern University in 1855. The University of Chicago was founded by the Baptists two years later.

A committee from the congregations of the First and Second Presbyterian churches of Chicago rode the new railroad north in 1856, and persuaded the conductor to let them off between Highland Park and Lake Bluff. Struck by the beauty of the place, they named it Lake Forest on the spot and determined to establish three schools there: an academy for young men, a young ladies' seminary, and a college.

They formed a stock company, the Lake Forest Association, and purchased 2,300 acres—50 to be set aside for the schools. Lind University, named for Sylvester Lind who pledged $100,000, was chartered on February 13, 1857.

Lind, a realtor, lumberman, and insurance executive, had dreamed of establishing a theological seminary for years. But he lost his fortune in the panic of 1857, and was unable to fulfill his pledge. His dream of a theological seminary was usurped by Cyrus

McCormick, who founded the McCormick Theological Seminary in Chicago. Lind remained a beloved figure in Lake Forest, however, and served four terms as mayor.

Soon after its formation, the association hired Jed Hotchkiss, a landscape architect. Hotchkiss laid out the town in park-style, following the natural curve of the ravines.

Lake Forest Academy opened in 1858 and the girls' school, which was the antecedent of Ferry Hall, opened in 1860. A few college classes—elocution, Cicero, optics, and pneumatics—began to be taught in the fall of 1859, but when the Civil War decimated both the faculty and the student body they were discontinued. Although a new charter changed the name to Lake Forest University in 1865, nothing really got off the ground until Mary Farwell's daughter was ready to graduate from a Chicago high school 11 years later.

Mary Farwell, wife of the prominent

Below: Teachers in Lake County chose to meet for their institute on August 12, 1881, at the oldest school in Lake County, built in 1836, the same year Vardin's Grove was settled. The school, 100 feet west of Milwaukee Avenue where Cook Avenue is now, was a log school with a large veranda in front. "The Block School," as it was known, gained a second story and clapboarding in 1860. After A.B. Cook bought the site in 1886, a section of "The Brick School" (Central School) was built. Courtesy, Libertyville-Mundelein Historical Society

Above: *The County House, or county poor farm, was a forerunner of today's Winchester House extended-care facility operated by Lake County at the same site on North Milwaukee Avenue, Libertyville. Charles A. Appley, a prominent Libertyville native who worked for the building of the poor farm, was named its assistant superintendent in 1869, and superintendent in 1879. Courtesy, Libertyville-Mundelein Historical Society*

senator, C.B. Farwell, did not want her daughter to go east to college. Instead, she got behind the Lake Forest Association and saw that the Lake Forest school got going on a permanent basis—and surprisingly, as a coeducational institution. Classes began on September 7, 1876, with a faculty of three. An educated and cultured woman, Mary Farwell personally financed the educations of many of the early students at the college.

Heated debates on temperance raged across the nation in the decades preceding the Civil War, and Lake County was no exception. Washington Temperance Societies, which utilized the emotionalism of revival meetings to promote temperance, became popular around the country. A Lake County group met on October 9, 1845, at the Methodist church in Libertyville with Seth Paine as president, and committees formed around the county. Even in Oak Precinct around Dwyer's stage stop, where feelings ran high against prohibition, a small group was organized consisting of B.P. Swain, M.C. Maguire, and Josiah Wright.

Responding to the public sentiment that had preceded the formation of the new societies, the county board ordered in September that no more grocery licenses be issued for spiritous liquors. Counter pressures caused them to pull back somewhat in January, and declare that grocery licenses would be granted to any "house of entertainment with four beds and stabling for eight horses." This, of course, brought a howl of protest from the Washington Temperance Society.

Prohibition was spreading rapidly across the country, however, and by 1855 more than half of the states were dry. Illinois put the issue to the voters in a special election on June 4, 1855. According to Vliet, Prohibition was rejected by 54 percent of the voters statewide but in Lake County it passed, winning 74 percent of the vote. Shields was the only township that voted against it.

Already at fever pitch, abolitionists were further inflamed by the passage of the Fugitive Slave Law of 1850, which held that escaped slaves were not free by virtue of crossing over into a free state. They could be captured and returned to their owners regardless of where they were apprehended. James Dorsey, in his book *Up South,* suggests that this may have been the reason that settler Amos Bennett, his wife, and two children were listed in the 1850 census, but had disappeared by 1860 when the next census was taken.

Even before the passage of the odious law, groups had begun to form in Lake County. On February 17, 1846, the Lake County Anti-Slavery Society was organized in Antioch. On March 3 a convention of the Lake County Liberty Association was held in Libertyville, and in June a large religious convocation was called in Half Day to protest both slavery and intemperance. That same month Richard Murphy spoke on abolition at a rally at the courthouse.

Halsey reports that the 1846 call for volunteers for the Mexican War fell on deaf ears in Lake County, to the credit of its citizens since "the war with Mexico was a slaveholders' filibustering attack . . . with a view to the creation of a larger South . . ."

Henry W. Blodgett, an attorney and later a federal judge, was one of the prominent abolitionists in the area. For six months in 1847, just two years after he had arrived in Waukegan, he published an anti-slavery newspaper, the *Lake County Visitor.* According to Haines, in 1852 Blodgett was the first to be elected to the Illinois General Assembly as an anti-slavery man. Later he helped to organize the Republican party in Illinois, and is believed to have been part of the inner circle that was instrumental in securing Abraham Lincoln's nomination to the presidency.

Blodgett was elected to the state senate in 1858 and appointed to the federal bench in 1869. It is a widely held belief that his home was one of the stops on the underground railroad, which helped fugitive slaves escape to Canada. These stops are difficult to document, however, because as Dorsey points out: "No one talked very much about this railroad which left no tracks."

The Congregationalist churches were outspoken in their denunciation of slavery, however, and on December 2, 1859, the Millburn Congregational Church openly passed a resolution denouncing it. Earlier, the Fox Lake Emancipation Society had passed a resolution

specifically denouncing the Fugitive Slave Law. Seth Paine of Lake Zurich was a known abolitionist as was the Reverend Joseph Payne of the Ivanhoe Congregational Church, and throughout the county there were stations on the underground railroad.

Sarah Blanchard Stafford, as an older woman reminiscing about her family's pioneer days in Warren Township, recalled her father, Phillip Blanchard, helping runaway slaves.

Another personal account comes from the diary of Jeduthan Talcott, son of Asahel Talcott, who came to Half Day soon after Captain Wright. Civic-minded young Talcott recorded that between 1850 and 1854 he attended abolitionist meetings, another meeting at which he pledged $50 toward the building of a road from Port Clinton to Half Day, and a third at which he bought one share of railroad stock.

It is interesting to note that on February 2, 1859, a few weeks after Waukegan was incorporated as a city, the renowned former slave Frederick Douglass lectured there on the "Races of Man."

On an April evening just a year later, Abraham Lincoln was the featured speaker at a political rally in Dickinson's Hall. Mayor Elisha Ferry and his wife, Sarah, entertained the Springfield lawmaker for supper at their home. The three of them then walked to the hall on the bluff overlooking the lake, where a modest crowd had gathered.

Lincoln had just begun to speak when a fire broke out on the flats, the flames clearly visible from the windows. Ferry tried to calm the crowd, assuring them there was no danger from the fire. Lincoln started his speech again but by this time most of the crowd had drifted out, lured by the excitement of the fire. According to a *Chicago Tribune* report, Lincoln said: "Guess we might as well go to the fire, too."

Waukeganites never did get to hear what Lincoln had to say because that ended the meeting. After the fire he returned to the Ferrys' home on the northwest corner of Julian and Utica streets, spent the night, and left town the next day. Had the rally been held only six months later—after Abraham Lincoln had been nominated to the presidency—the *Tribune* reporter speculated, "The whole of

Below: An early and prominent abolitionist was Henry W. Blodgett, an attorney and federal judge whose home was said to be a stop on the Underground Railway. It is also said that Blodgett, who helped organize the Republican party in Illinois, hosted Abraham Lincoln in this house overnight when candidate Lincoln sought Blodgett's help to gain Lake County support for his presidential bid. The house was demolished in the 1940s. Courtesy, Waukegan Historical Society

Lake County would have been present and stayed to the end come fire or high water."

Little noted or scarcely remembered is the fact that Stephen Douglas, who ran against Lincoln, also spoke in Waukegan on a stopover during the campaign.

Lake County voted overwhelmingly for Lincoln, giving him 2,402 votes to Douglas' 962, and on March 4, 1861, he was inaugurated as the 16th president of the United States. Scarcely a month later the nation was embroiled in a bitter Civil War, destined to bring profound changes in the lives of all Americans.

Three days after Fort Sumter was fired on, Lincoln sent out a call for troops, and on the fourth day a mass meeting was called in

Waukegan by Mayor David Ballentine. After many stirring speeches, young men rushed to sign up, and just a week later 84 volunteers left Waukegan to be part of the Zouave Regiment. They were the first company to arrive in Chicago.

The recruiting drum continued to roll across the county, and to encourage enlistments the county board voted several appropriations for bounties for volunteers and funds to help care for their dependents while they were away. Members of the Lake County Union Rifle Guards were recruited from the southwestern part of the county. Other men went individually to Chicago to join the Irish Brigade. The 37th regiment of Lake Countians was one of the last to be mustered out—

serving almost five years and not returning home until May 31, 1866. Historian Charles Partridge said: "Few troops were called on to march as many miles."

By 1862 the war had lost its glamour. Everyone knew there was more pain than pomp involved in soldiering. Nevertheless when another call went out for volunteers, Lake County recruiters hoping to raise one company raised four—Companies B, C, D, and G of the 96th regiment—with the stipulation that they not be sworn in until after the harvest in the fall. When they left by train from Waukegan, the patriotic ladies of the town gave them pin and needle cushions. They fought in the desperate battle of Chickamauga on Lookout Mountain, and in the Atlanta campaign.

Out of a population of 19,000 Lake County sent 2,000 men to war, 1,600 of whom were volunteers. Four hundred never returned.

Behind the statistics were the names and the faces. Captain Evangelist Gillmore of Avon, a 26-year-old farmer and teacher, was mortally wounded at Kenesaw Mountain, Georgia, just a month after his request for a leave in order to settle financial affairs at home was denied.

Sergeant Edward Murray of Newport Township was wounded at Chickamauga by a bullet that paralyzed his legs, another that went through his arm, and a third that lodged in his hip. He lay all day on enemy lines and according to reports, "was sent home a wreck of the strong man who entered the service."

Henry P. Ostrander and his son, Henry W. Ostrander, of Rockland (Lake Bluff) enlisted together. The younger man fell ill and died before reaching the front, as did many other soldiers who contracted pneumonia, typhoid, or measles in overcrowded, unsanitary camps. Henry P. was wounded and discharged.

John Williams, a Welchman also of Rockland, enlisted in the Eighth Illinois Cavalry at the age of 41, lost an arm at Gettysburg, and returned home to become Waukegan lighthouse keeper, still retaining enough stamina at age 51 to take a second wife 30 years his junior.

Lyston Howe of Waukegan enlisted as a non-combatant drummer at the age of 10, and is considered the youngest person to have served in the Civil War. Not much older, his 13-year-old brother, Orion, also enlisted as a drummer and was cited for heroism at the Battle of Vicksburg for carrying ammunition to the men on the front lines.

Sergeant Calvin Durand of Lake Forest was taken prisoner and sent to Andersonville. He wrote: "After entering the stockade . . . the sight that met our eyes was simply appalling and our hearts dropped within us. It seemed to me that we were really in the land of the inferno." He later returned, and in 1891 was elected mayor of Lake Forest.

Church bells rang out across the county when Lee surrendered to Grant at Appomattox on April 8, 1865. People were wild with joy.

Left: *One of the youngest soldiers in the Union army was Waukegan's Lyston D. Howe. According to records, he enlisted at the age of 10 years, nine months, but was discharged because "he could not endure the fatigue of marching." (Another version indicates he was discharged because he contracted measles.) He rejoined four months later to take part in Sherman's March on Atlanta. Howe was reportedly only four feet, two inches tall. Lyston's father and older brother, Orion, age 13, were also in the army. Courtesy, Lake County Museum*

Below: *In November 1870 Waukegan's Genesee Street was an unpaved byway for horse-drawn wagons. The downtown area catered to the times, providing livery stables, harness and trunk makers, and a lumber yard. Courtesy, Waukegan Historical Society*

Right: *Harvest 1913 was a popular time for youngsters visiting Selter's Summer Resort and Sportsman's Lodge on Grass Lake Road and Springwell, Antioch. The rural character of the area and proximity to the Chain O'Lakes drew a brisk summer trade. The resorts began with residents taking in a few boarders, generally from Chicago, and adding on rooms as their popularity increased. Selter's closed right after World War I, as Prohibition came into effect. Courtesy, Lake County Museum*

CHAPTER 3

HIGH TIDE

Young men far from home, fighting a war, dream of little else than returning to find everything exactly as they left it. But that is seldom the reality. When the boys in blue came marching back to Lake County, it was already in a state of flux.

Less than two months after the guns were stilled at Appomattox, the first execution in the county's history took place in the courthouse in Waukegan—a sign, perhaps, of the growing complexity of life there.

The *Waukegan Weekly Gazette* reported on July 1, 1865, that on June 30, William Bell was hanged inside the courthouse in front of the courtroom door for the murder of Ruth Briden in 1863. Witnesses included the 12 jurors, several clergymen, and reporters from Chicago newspapers as well as local journalists. The prisoner, the *Gazette* said, was allowed to speak for an hour during which he proclaimed his innocence and expressed the hope that this would also be the last execution in the county.

Just days after the war ended, the First National Bank of Waukegan opened with a capitalization of $50,000 and Charles R. Steele as president.

The 1865 census showed a population of 18,660 in the county, with 3,905 children in 110 schools—a far cry from the first log schoolhouse built in Libertyville through contributions from settlers a scant 35 years earlier.

Politically, voters in the county continued to support the Republican party, giving Abraham Lincoln 2,403 votes (one more than he had received in the previous election) in 1864. Shields and Grant townships still voted Democratic, but by a small majority. This followed the national trend pointed out by S.L. Mayer in *The Almanac of American History.* The Democrats, he said, represented the South and the immigrants who had begun crowding into the cities. The Republicans gained strength in small towns and farms where "people shuddered at the thought of

Below: Mineral springs in the ravines of Waukegan offered promise for entrepreneurs of a burgeoning "health resort" business. This photo, taken in May 1874, shows the Glen Flora Springs, owned by C.C. Parks. The water was offered as a "Water Cure" and reportedly was sold throughout the world. Courtesy, Lake County Museum

these huddled masses yearning to breathe free . . ."

From December 13, 1869, to May 13, 1870, delegates met in Springfield to draft a new state constitution. Elijah Haines was the delegate from Lake County. The state had already ratified the 15th Amendment to the U.S. Constitution granting blacks the right to vote, and convention delegates did not hesitate over striking "white" from the clause which had previously read "every white male over the age of 21."

Despite arguments presented by Haines for also striking "male," his fellow delegates did not agree and women remained disenfranchised.

Other changes included the establishment of a public school system and the enlargement of the state supreme court, with Lake County in the seventh district. Judge William K. McAllister of Chicago was elected, and he served until 1875.

Promptly after his election McAllister moved to Waukegan, where he lived on a large tract which today is the site of Roosevelt Park. The beautiful wooded hills and ravines contained five mineral springs, and the judge hoped to turn the property into a health resort. Indeed, earlier the Glen Flora Springs (on Sheridan Road) had been dedicated and a hotel was built there. But although the railroad established a stop there, dreams of promoting Waukegan as a great health resort never materialized.

In other judicial matters Henry Blodgett was appointed a Federal Judge for the Northern District of Illinois in 1870, a post he held until 1893 when he resigned to act as counsel for the United States before the Behring Sea Arbitrators.

When the glare from the Chicago Fire filled the night sky on October 8, 1871, Waukegan volunteer firemen, headed by Lewis Crabtree, hastened to aid their neighbors. Waukegan could not send its only engine, so the city of Racine, Wisconsin, loaded one onto the next train bound for Waukegan. When the train arrived, Waukegan firemen got aboard with 700 feet of hose, traveled to Chicago, and spent two days battling the blaze.

Although Lake County was still largely

rural at the close of the Civil War, rules and regulations began to define and refine life. On March 1, 1867, a law was passed forbidding owners of sheep and hogs to let them run loose. Fines were assessed at five dollars per head, with three-fifths of the revenue marked for a soldiers' monument to be built near the courthouse. In Waukegan there were ordinances prohibiting fast driving, leaving horses unhitched, and throwing ashes in the streets.

Wolves were a big problem for farmers, and March 1868 saw the "great wolf drive." Some 350 men with guns closed in on Nelson Landon's farm in Benton Township and killed a grand total of three wolves.

By 1873 all established roads in the county were declared public highways and their care was given to a road commissioner in each township, a job not without its perils. Ela Township pioneer John Robertson, while serving as road commissioner, was shot and killed by an irate farmer when he tried to open a road through the man's farm.

Road taxes were assessed at 40 cents on $100 of property valuation, and each person could work out his levy if he wanted to at $1.50 per day. Men usually were called out after corn planting for a week or two, and looked forward to the hiatus from farm chores as a congenial outing. In 1877 the system was changed and road taxes were required to be paid in money. There was such a public outcry that a return to the original system was effected in 1879. Finally, in 1883, the labor system of paying taxes was abolished once and for all.

The *Gazette* noted in February 1871 that fewer bushels of wheat and oats were being shipped from Waukegan, and suggested that they consider promoting themselves as a suburb like Lake Forest and Highland Park.

When the Highland Park Building Company, a land development group represented locally by Frank Hawkins, purchased the Port Clinton Land Corporation from Walter Gurnee there was little there, the original Port Clinton settlement having failed to thrive when the railroad bypassed them. But with a railroad stop now assured, the building company set out to attract commuters. Within 10 months the community had grown to 10 substantial houses, and a number of winding roads

had been laid out. Stores and churches soon followed and, when the city was incorporated in 1869, Hawkins became the first mayor.

One of the incorporators of Highland Park, the Reverend W.W. Everts, bought property for the settlement of his family and friends west and north of Port Clinton. He called his settlement Highwood. The Baptist minister intended his community to be home to people of moderate means, but because it was not accessible to jobs it did not immediately prosper. The building of Fort Sheridan adjacent to the village in 1887 finally provided employment, and began to attract a working class.

The first settlers were mostly Scandina-

Facing page, top: *Central School in Waukegan was the first school in the city, built on land purchased in 1865 at Utica and Clayton streets, where the public library is today. In 1870 the schools were graded and the first high school met at Central School. Central School burned in 1889 and was rebuilt within a year. By 1896 there were 167 high school students, but a separate high school (the South Building of Waukegan East High School) was not built until 1905. Courtesy, E.W. Plonien Collection, Waukegan Historical Society*

Left: *Chauncey J. Jones was president of the First National Bank of Waukegan, which opened its doors just a few days after the end of the Civil War. Jones, who joined the bank in 1870, took over from Nelson Steele, son of founder Charles R. Steele, and was president until his retirement in 1925. Except for Jones, members of the Steele family held the office of president for more than a century. Courtesy, Waukegan Historical Society*

Far left: *Waukegan couldn't send its only fire engine to aid in fighting the Great Chicago Fire in 1871, but it did send firefighters and 700 feet of hose. This horse-drawn steam pumper was used in Waukegan in the 1870s. Courtesy, Waukegan Historical Society*

driving force in the Women's Christian Temperance Union, which was founded in 1874. The meetings also drew leading preachers of the day. The number of families attracted to the beautiful lakefront setting continued to grow and many began moving out of tents into more substantial dwellings, with some eventually establishing year-round residences in the community. Finally, in 1895, Lake Bluff was incorporated as a village.

Temperance and religion played major parts in the histories of many towns in Lake County, but in none more graphically than in Zion, which was founded as a theocracy by John Alexander Dowie.

A preacher and faith healer, born in Scotland and reared in Australia, Dowie came to the United States in 1888. By 1896, when he organized the Christian Catholic Church, he was drawing crowds of up to 6,000 at his tabernacle in Chicago. He promised his followers a dramatic surprise to be revealed at a watch service on New Year's Eve, 1899. As revelers across the city rang in the new year, Dowie drew the curtain off a large plat map of a city he proposed to build 35 miles north

Above: *John Alexander Dowie (center), founder of Zion, organized his Christian Catholic Church in 1896. Four years later, this dynamic preacher and faith healer had purchased a 10-square-mile area about 35 miles north of Chicago, and the theocracy was begun. Dowie, shown flanked by his son and daughter, died in 1907, his vision of an earthly Utopia in shambles. His son, Gladstone, fell into disfavor, was disinherited by his father, and later became an Episcopalian minister. Daughter Esther died in a fire after accidentally overturning an alcohol lamp she was using to set her hair. Courtesy, Waukegan News-Sun*

vian. The first Italian, Joseph Ori, arrived on the scene in 1906. Almost immediately scores of his countrymen from the northern Italian province of Modena poured in, giving Highwood the Italian character it retains to this day. Many other Italians came looking for work when the mines closed in southern Illinois, and a good number found it on the estates springing up along the North Shore.

Lake Bluff, on the other hand, began as a Methodist summer camp meeting site thanks to the zeal and affluence of Solomon and Clara Thatcher of River Forest. The Thatchers purchased 200 acres of lakefront property in 1873 and turned it over to the Lake Bluff Camp Meeting Association, which they had been instrumental in founding. By the time the first meeting opened on July 6, 1876, to a large enthusiastic crowd of campers, a hotel to accommodate 100, a dining room to seat 300, and a tabernacle-tent to seat 3,000 had been erected. Modeled after the renowned Chautauqua, New York, resort, the camp meetings caught the attention of celebrities such as Frances Willard, a friend of Clara Thatcher's and a

of Chicago.

For months prior to his announcement, Dowie's agents had secretly been buying up land in a 10-mile square area for the Zion Land Investment Association. On July 14, 1900, Dowie turned the first spadeful of earth in the construction of a temple on the Zion site. Surveyors and road crews led by Burton J. Ashley, a civil engineer who had worked on the Art Institute of Chicago, began working in the area. To provide jobs city-owned industries were started, most notably a lace factory which was imported from England along with some of its skilled supervisory personnel. By July 15, 1901, lots were offered for lease to the faithful for 1,100 years, and in their anxiety to become citizens of the new city, they pitched tents and began to build their houses.

Elijah Hospice, one of the largest frame-buildings in the country, was constructed to house single male workers. Parks and schools were included in the master plan. Dowie was the absolute ruler of all he surveyed, and nothing that went on in Zion escaped his attention and direction. He also began calling himself "Elijah, the Restorer," and built for himself

and his family a 25-room house costing $75,000 which stood in sharp contrast to the modest homes of his followers.

Things came to a head in 1905. Financial affairs in Zion were in a state of collapse, yet Dowie persisted in pursuing his dream of establishing another settlement in Mexico. Industries were in receivership, people were out of work, and there was hunger and hardship everywhere. Wilbur Glenn Voliva, who had been laboring for the Christian Catholic Church in Australia, returned to Zion while Dowie was out of the country. Voliva took over the reins of church and city, and held on to them with an iron fist for 35 years. He is best remembered for advocating the theory that the earth is flat.

Dowie died in his home, Shiloh House, on March 9, 1907, a sick and broken man. Whether he was a charlatan or a naive dreamer is still debated. There is no doubt that he was a dynamic speaker, a leader of men, and in many ways a visionary. He established an eight-hour workday in the industries of Zion; he spoke of the equality of man and lashed out at racism; and he advocated the free and compulsory education of children. Always ready to explore new ideas, he once said, "I know not the possibilities of electricity. It is possible that it may yet convey the face of the speaker . . ."

According to Jabez Taylor, who wrote *The Development of the City of Zion,* in an age when government was by special interests—railroads, banks, steel companies, and the mining industry—small businessmen, laborers, and farmers all had grievances. It is no

Below left: *After 75 years, the Zion Hotel's usefulness had ceased. Despite numerous efforts by the town and the Zion Park District, which purchased the hotel, to save the majestic structure, plans were made for its demolition. Potential developers shied away, fearing the wooden structure was a fire-trap, was too costly, or development including a restaurant would not succeed in the town where liquor sales were prohibited. At long last, the wrecking crane began its work, saving only the striking dome and rotunda, the only reminder of the once-proud Elijah Hospice. Courtesy,* Waukegan News-Sun

Below: *When John Alexander Dowie, the founder of the City of Zion, died in 1907, his dream of a religious utopia was already crumbling. Finances were collapsing, and attempts were being made to set up another "City of God" in Mexico. Dowie died in his 25-room home in Zion, no longer in power after his henchman, Wilbur Glenn Voliva, had taken over the city. Courtesy, Waukegan Historical Society*

in the Midwest. In 1891 Washburn-Moen merged with American Steel and Wire Company of Illinois to become American Steel and Wire Company of New Jersey, which 10 years later was one of the organizations that banded together to become U.S. Steel Corporation. The local plant continued as a subsidiary until 1952, when it became a division of U.S. Steel. From the onset they were a major employer, hiring 700 people soon after they opened.

Michael Hussey, who in 1906 was known as the coal baron of northern Illinois according to an article by Barbara Apple in *The News-Sun,* built the first electric-generating plant in Lake County. He is said to have employed 200 people, and annually processed 125,000 tons of coal at his yards on the Waukegan lakefront.

Another early industry was the National Envelope Company in North Chicago, opened in 1904. Goelitz Candy Company, which in the 1980s became famous for the Jelly Belly jelly beans favored by President Ronald Reagan, moved to North Chicago in 1912. Pfanstiehl Electrical Laboratories was incorporated in 1907 by Carl Pfanstiehl, a brilliant inventor who did early work with tungsten. By 1918 he

Above: *Wilbur Glenn Voliva, who took over as general overseer of Zion in 1905, kept rigid control of the reins of the City for 35 years. He brought motion pictures into the religious city, but he previewed them personally to check their suitability, and the movies were shown in the Zion Tabernacle.* Courtesy, Waukegan News-Sun

wonder that these people, looking for a Utopia, flocked to Zion where Dowie promised profit-sharing and an environment free from the corruption of the city—the same things sought by the more affluent along the North Shore.

Industry, meanwhile, was moving into Waukegan and North Chicago, which was established in 1891 when a real estate syndicate purchased farmlands and offered 15,000 lots for sale. "No saloons" was the trademark of the town then called South Waukegan. It was incorporated in 1895 and its name was changed to North Chicago in 1908.

The Besley Brewery, which used good spring water in its product; the U.S. Sugar Refinery on Market Street, which was the scene of a spectacular explosion in 1903; and the U.S. Starch Works were the chief industries in Waukegan in 1890, when Washburn-Moen Manufacturing Company decided to locate a plant in what was to become South Waukegan.

A manufacturer of nails, fence, barbed wire, and wire net, Washburn-Moen was out to capture the burgeoning agricultural trade

had left the company, and with anti-German feeling running high in the United States the name of the company was changed to Fansteel Products Company. Ironically, Pfanstiehl is a Dutch name.

Railroads and industry went hand in hand. None was more important to Waukegan's economy than the Elgin, Joliet and East-

Left: *If all had gone right, the Besley Brewery at 200 S. Utica Street might have made Waukegan the "beer capital of the world." Founded in 1853, the brewery, one of the city's earliest industries, used Waukegan's spring water to brew malt liquors that were sold throughout the U.S. and exported abroad. The four-wheeled brewery wagons with their double-horse teams were a familiar sight at the turn of the century, until Prohibition put the brewery out of business. Courtesy, Waukegan Historical Society*

Below: *Waukegan's Sugar Refinery, the more popular name for the Corn Products Refining Company on South Market Street, was the scene of a massive explosion and fire on November 25, 1912. The factory's "starch house" exploded, killing 14 and injuring 19, making it the state's first test of the recently passed Workmen's compensation Act. The company reportedly had to pay nearly $80,000 in liability claims. Courtesy, Waukegan Historical Society*

ern Railroad, a freight line that linked the city to important industrial points south. Population had actually declined between 1870 and 1880, and growth was static when the city council granted rights to the company first known as the Waukegan and Southwestern Railroad. The first train came into Waukegan on December 31, 1889. Often referred to as the Outer Belt Line, it originally went from Waukegan to Porter, Indiana, skirting Elgin and Joliet. Service was later extended to the industrial centers of South Chicago and Hammond and Gary, Indiana, but it did not actually reach Elgin until 1962. From the beginning, the EJ&E interchanged with all rail lines leaving and entering Chicago.

Lake Zurich, a center for German immigrants in the 1850s and 1860s, was also on the EJ&E route. This enhanced its reputation as a shipping center for cattle, hogs, and dairy products.

Six years after the EJ&E began service, the Bluff City Electric Interurban Street Railway Company began running trolley cars from North and Franklin streets in Waukegan to North Chicago. By 1898 it was operating as far south as Highland Park, and its name had been changed to the Chicago and Milwaukee Electric Railway. New cars were ordered that year, and it was reported their arrival in town was a gala affair. Most of the town turned out to watch as the cars were hauled up the hill

Below: *Washburn-Moen
Manufacturing Company
opened in South Waukegan
in 1890. Shortly afterward,
its nails, fence, barbed
wire, and other products
were being transported nationwide. This train, loaded
with "Waukegan Barbed
Wire," made its way from
the Western Works at
Waukegan to San Antonio,
Texas, in July 1895. The
company merged with
American Steel and Wire
Co. of Illinois and 10 years
later became a part of U.S.
Steel Corp. At its peak in
the 1950s the plant em-
ployed 3,000. It shut down
in 1979. Courtesy, Wauke-
gan Historical Society*

two years of college, reported for classes. By 1919 the transition had been made to a four-year college, which was chartered as Barat College. In the same solid, red brick building erected early in the century, the college continues to educate—men as well as women today.

People to power the industries began to pour into Waukegan and North Chicago, just as they were pouring into the country. Waukegan's population in 1890 was 4,915. By 1900 it had jumped to 9,426 and by 1910 to 16,069.

Historian Arthur M. Schlesinger, Jr., said that between 1881 and 1890 more than 5 million immigrants arrived in this country, their port of entry at that time being Castle Garden. Beginning in 1892, millions more crossed over to the promised land through Ellis Island. Those who made their way to Lake County gave Waukegan and North Chicago the unique, ethnic, melting-pot character still retained today.

The first group of Finns came in 1889 and it was the Finnish women, incensed about the price and quality of milk, who formed the first milk cooperative. Eventually the movement grew to include grocery stores, meat markets, and the present Consumers Cooperative Credit Union.

Fleeing massacre by Turks in their homeland, Armenians began arriving in 1885. Croatians, Slovenes, Slovaks, and Lithuanians all settled on the south side of Waukegan,

Above: *Only five people were hurt when two cars of the Chicago and Milwaukee Electric Railroad collided at the Edison Court Station in Waukegan on September 15, 1912. A local car was heading east on Washington Street, approaching the main crossing, when it was struck squarely by a car on the main line. Courtesy, E.W. Plonien Collection, Waukegan Historical Society*

Above left: *In this circa 1910 photo, wires crisscrossed over Waukegan's Genesee Street (looking north at the intersection of Washington Street), as the changing methods of transportation came to town. Trolleys had been installed for more than 15 years, and horseless carriages were becoming more numerous on the brick-paved streets. Courtesy, Waukegan Historical Society*

from the North Western freight yards by four-horse teams.

A year later service was extended to Evanston, and by 1905 trains were running between Lake Bluff and Libertyville, and Mundelein to the west. In 1908 the electric line connected Milwaukee and Chicago along the shoreline, but it was not until 1926 that a second line to the west, known as the Skokie Valley Route, was established. By that time the name of the railroad had been changed to Chicago, North Shore and Milwaukee Railroad. It continued to operate until 1963.

One of the early stops on the shoreline route was identified by its sign as Sacred Heart. A Catholic order of nuns, the Society of the Sacred Heart decided to move its seminary for young women from Chicago to Lake Forest in 1904. In the first year 66 boarders, ranging from the first grade through the first

Above: *Horse-drawn sleighs were about all that managed to move along Genesee Street in Waukegan during the heavy snows of 1888. At the corner is Pearce's Drug Store, long a fixture in downtown Waukegan. Dr. W.S. Pearce founded the store in 1855 and practiced medicine there, while his daughter Beatrice, also a physician, had an office upstairs. Courtesy, Waukegan Historical Society*

Right: *One of Waukegan's more prominent physicians, Dr. Vincent Price, arrived in 1858. He made a name for himself as the inventor of Dr. Price's Cream Baking Powder. Perhaps his interest in chemical experiments is manifested in his grandson and namesake, Hollywood star Vincent Price, whose abilities as a gourmet cook are almost as well known as his acting talents. Dr. Price's Queen Anne-style home on Grand Avenue, Waukegan, was converted to apartments and still stands today. Courtesy, E.W. Plonien Collection, Waukegan Historical Society*

within walking distance of the wire mill and usually with their church at the center of their neighborhood. They often established their own savings and loan associations and formed fraternal societies with large halls, such as the Lithuanian Auditorium and the Slovenic National Home, which served as meeting places.

Many Greeks settled on the west side of North Chicago, according to Peggy Moraitis writing in *Historical Highlights of the Waukegan Area*. Poles also clustered in North Chicago around 14th Street.

Coming first to work in the sugar refinery and later in the wire mill, the Swedes built their homes along McAlister Avenue and established the renowned Swedish Glee Club.

These immigrants mostly settled south of Belvidere Street, where their blue collar status, multiplicity of languages, and diversity of ethnic customs gave the area an identity apart from the rest of the city. This bonded them into a kind of fraternity and in later years they wore the fact that they had "come from the South Side" like a badge of honor.

Increased population brought demands for better health care. Since Dr. Jesse Foster had set up shop in Libertyville in 1836, caring for the sick and injured and dispensing medicine out of his home, other doctors had opened practices. Among them were Dr. David Cory, who built a log house in Waukegan in 1838 and later served as a president of the village board; Dr. Fremont Knight, who moved from

Libertyville to Waukegan in 1895, and was the American Steel & Wire Company's doctor for many years and coroner for 16; Dr. Vincent Price, grandfather of his namesake the popular Hollywood actor and inventor of baking powder, which brought him fame and fortune; and Dr. Beatrice Pearce, who practiced from an office above her father's pharmacy in downtown Waukegan.

Finally in 1891 the Lake County Hospital Association was formed, purchasing a residence at 720 North Avenue in Waukegan which it converted to a six-bed hospital. In five years, demand necessitated a move to a larger residence two blocks south. On that site at the corner of North and Franklin streets, a hospital building was erected in 1904 thanks to a donation of $21,000 by Jane McAlister, for whom the new hospital was named.

In 1908 tuberculosis, or consumption, was a dreaded disease against which the only known weapons were fresh air day and night, good water, and nourishing food. That year the Lake County Tuberculosis Institute was founded to treat the disease as well as collect and disseminate information. A tent colony in Waukegan, where patients could get a maximum of fresh air, came under the jurisdiction of the institute. According to the book *Waukegan's Legacy*, a former patient remembered it as a "cold, lonely place where there was no medicine, only lots of fresh air, lots of milk, and fresh eggs." Although medical technology advanced and people began to be treated in sanatoriums, Lake County had no treatment facility until 1939, when the Tuberculosis Sanatorium was built in Waukegan. Designed by local architect William Ganster, it was cited for excellence of design. Today the building is used by the Lake County Health Department.

Industrialization spawned the labor

men stepped in and offered the government 172 acres of choice land on Lake Michigan, just south of North Chicago, for one dollar.

The flag was raised on July 1, 1911, and two days later the first recruit walked through the gates. On October 28, 1911, the station was dedicated by President William Taft. By 1917 there were 39 brick buildings, and during the First World War more than 100,000 men were trained at Great Lakes Naval Station.

Previous to that, activity increased at both posts during the Spanish-American War, which lasted from April 25 to August 12, 1898. The treaty which granted Cuba its independence from Spain, and put Puerto Rico, Guam, and the Philippines under U.S. jurisdiction, was signed on December 10, 1898. One government official is supposed to have

Left: *Jane Strang McAlister started with little cash when she and her husband moved from Canada to build a thriving sheep farm in Newport Township. On her death in October 1903 at the age of 86, she willed her personal estate, valued at $100,000, to various philanthropic causes, including the First Presbyterian Church in Waukegan and the Lake County Hospital Association, which named the Jane McAlister Hospital for her. Courtesy, Waukegan Historical Society*

movement, marked by the organization of the Federation of Organized Trades and Labor Unions of the U.S. (forerunner of the American Federation of Labor) by Samuel Gompers in 1881. The railway strike in 1877 and the Haymarket Riot in Chicago in 1886 prompted a group of wealthy Chicago businessmen and financiers to purchase land adjacent to Highwood, which they presented to the federal government for the establishment of a military post. They reasoned that this garrison would serve as protection against any further outbreaks of violence. The first troops arrived in 1887 and a series of architecturally significant buildings was soon erected. One of these buildings was the Fort Sheridan Tower, named for the popular Civil War general, Philip Sheridan. It was modeled after the campanile in St. Mark's Square in Venice and originally stood 227 feet high. Among the early officers assigned to Fort Sheridan was the then newly commissioned Second Lieutenant George S. Patton, Jr., in 1909.

Soon after the turn of the century, the Merchants Club of Chicago was influential in securing a second military post for Lake County. Congressman George Edmund Foss, Illinois representative of the 10th congressional district, commissioned a study to determine the number of Midwestern enlistees in the Navy, and following it, the secretary of the Navy appointed a board to select a site on the Great Lakes for a training station. Business-

called it a "neat little war," but to the 5,000 soldiers and sailors nationwide who lost their lives, it was not so neat. It is interesting to note, however, that more than 90 percent of the casualties were from disease. One was Ben Jones of Waukegan, who died of yellow fever.

While it lasted the conflict elicited a burst of patriotism, although the *Waukegan Daily Gazette* reported that one Waukegan woman had announced that her daughter "had

Above: *A growing population at the turn of the century brought increased needs for social services in Waukegan. The Lake County Hospital Association, outgrowing its original six-bed hospital, built a four-story brick hospital at the corner of North and Franklin streets. Courtesy, Waukegan Historical Society*

Above: *By the time of
America's entry into World
War I, Great Lakes Naval
Training Station was home
to 39 brick buildings,
among them the barracks
being constructed here.
Some 100,000 men were
trained at the Lake County
facility during the war.
Photo by Harold G.
Mason. Courtesy, Wauke-
gan Historical Society*

The Great Depression forced the park to
close from 1932 to 1935, and the stock company died. It was replaced in 1936 by the not-
for-profit Ravinia Festival Association, which
in the years since has brought stars such as
Lotte Lehmann, Pablo Casals, Igor Stravin-
sky, and Duke Ellington to Lake County. In
1983 some 16,000 people gathered in the
pavilion and on the lawns to hear opera star
Luciano Pavarotti.

The western part of the county had remained largely rural, and the coming of the
railroads in the late 1800s and early 1900s
brought the development of a vast resort business as the well-to-do discovered the delights
of the lake region. The Wisconsin Central
(later the Soo Line) laid tracks to Antioch in
1886 and a year later extended them to Lake
Villa, where there was some initial difficulty
with a railroad bridge across a slough. Testing
the first tracks with a seven-car train, workmen were dismayed to see the bridge collapse
and the train disappear. Finally, timber and
gravel were hauled in and a firm roadbed built.

The Chicago, Milwaukee and St. Paul
Railroad inaugurated rail service to Libertyville in 1878, and in 1900 extended it to Fox
Lake. At that time the station called Fox Lake
was where Ingleside is now, and the present
Fox Lake was known as Nippersink. About
1901 the names were changed to their present
designations.

In 1911 a steam interurban, the Palatine, Lake Zurich and Wauconda, began haul-
ing passengers and mail between those towns
and linked them with lines from Palatine to
Chicago. Resorts ranging from beer bistros to
elegant multi-veranda hotels sprang up on the
shores of every lake, offering room and board,
boats and bait, bathing beaches, ball games,
and badminton. These hotels all sent carriages
to the depots to pick up incoming guests. Still
standing today is one of the grandest of the old
hotels, the Mineola on Fox Lake, which pre-
dates the railroad. In those early days guests
and goods often traveled by rail to McHenry,
and from there to Fox Lake in steam replicas
of the Ohio River paddleboats. The Mineola
is a 225-foot, four-story frame structure with
a tower. In its heyday it sported a two-story
veranda.

One of the highlights of a visit during

no intention of going to war as a nurse." Many
other Waukegan residents, however, rode ex-
cursion trains to Camp Tanner in Springfield
to visit local boys who were in training. The
paper reported that some 100,000 people from
all over the state visited the camp during the
brief war, a scene that was repeated at military
installations across the nation.

Life took on a more leisurely pace in the
early years of the twentieth century, and people found themselves with more time for amenities. By 1900, Schlesinger said, every major
city in the country had a symphony orchestra.
Soon after, Lake County had Ravinia.

The subdivision of Ravinia was annexed
to Highland Park in 1899. In 1902 A.C. Frost,
president of the North Shore line, purchased
36 acres bisected by the railroad with the express purpose of stimulating business for the
road. The first improvements included a
grandstand and baseball field, and a theater
with a pipe organ, restaurant, and dance
floors. In 1905 an outdoor pavilion was built,
and its first season featured barefoot dancing
by Ruth St. Denis, a Shakespearean group
performing *A Midsummer's Night Dream,*
and Ibsen plays. Baseball, however, never got
off the ground and soon was ruled out.

When the railroad went into receivership, local resident Frank McMullen, fearing
the park would be subdivided, organized a Ravinia stock company. Major symphony orchestras and operas were introduced. According to
the book *Ravinia: The Festival At Its Half
Century,* some of the greatest opera singers in
the world appeared at Ravinia from 1919 to
1931, due in great part to the vision of a major
stockholder and moving force, Louis Eckstein.

July and August was a trip to the lotus beds in Grass Lake, often on the passenger steamer, the *Mamie.* These fragrant, lemon-colored blooms, measuring 18 inches across and framed by great, round, green leaves protruding above the water, once covered the lake like a carpet. Promoters of the era claimed they were indigenous to Egypt, and unique to Lake County in the United States. Modern naturalists identify them as American Lotus, and say they can be found on other rivers and lakes in the Midwest. Floods, dredging, and motor boats have taken their toll in recent years but

the lotus can still be seen, mainly along the shoreline of Grass Lake.

Early pioneers had found an abundance of wild rice in Long Lake, which attracted migratory birds and fish—and this drew later-day sportsmen. A 1900 Milwaukee Road brochure touted Long Lake as "one of the finest bits of water in the entire system."

E.J. Lehmann, millionaire owner of the Fair Store in Chicago, was one of the first to recognize the commercial possibilities of the area. In 1883 he purchased an old hotel on a hill overlooking Cedar Lake in Lake Villa, and

Below: *In 1917, just six years after Great Lakes Naval Training Station was officially dedicated by President Taft, it already had the appearance of an active, bustling military base. The 172 acres of land, fronting Lake Michigan just south of North Chicago, were offered to the government for one dollar. Photo by Harold G. Mason. Courtesy, Waukegan Historical Society*

renamed it the Lake City Hotel. He then used his influence to persuade the railroad to establish service to Lake Villa. Unfortunately, due to his failing health and a fire at the hotel in 1915, his plans were never fully realized.

Nevertheless, Lehmann and his six children left an indelible stamp on the community. His home, occupied after his death by his daughter, Augusta, is now owned by the Central Baptist Children's Home. Son Edward built a mansion on 1,100 acres, which he called Longwood Farm. Son Ernst called his estate Lindenhurst; it has been subdivided and retains that name. Son Otto established Chesney Farm on the Fox Lake branch of his father's property and this, too, has been subdivided as Chesney Shores. Daughter Edith lived in a cottage on the original estate while her sister, Emilia, married an heir of the C.D. Peacock jewelry family. They and a number of their children all built grand houses on Deep Lake. All told, the Lehmann family at one time occupied some 2,000 acres of property in and around Lake Villa.

One of the few industries in the lakes region died out with the coming of refrigeration. But in the years around the turn of the century ice cutting was big business. Migratory workers were brought from Chicago and housed in dormitories while they used ice picks, ice axes, and sometimes horse-pulled saws to cut 100-pound blocks of ice. These were wrapped in straw and covered with sawdust, and could be stored in icehouses all summer long. Some blocks were cut up and sold to local consumers, but many tons were shipped to meatpackers at the stockyards in Chicago.

Historian John Halsey said that Armour and Company actually owned Round Lake, and 4,000 tons of ice were cut there each winter under the management of Frank Fenderson.

Although Halsey bemoaned the fact that "every class comes [to the resorts] and some places reek to heaven," recreation for the vast majority consisted of more simple pursuits closer to home. Baseball was a favorite summer activity. Bicycling became popular about 1890, and many also took up tennis at that time.

Libertyville, which was incorporated in 1882, hosted the highly popular Lake County fair for many years. In the early 1900s harness racing drew big crowds to the Mile Track at the corner of Park and Milwaukee avenues in Libertyville. Although the town was the site of a huge gravel mining operation (today Lake Minear) and a few small factories including Foulds Macaroni Company, according to Halsey it was "sufficiently off the lines of travel to retain that independent character as a country town which the larger towns and cities on the lakeshore have lost."

Urban problems such as poor working conditions, slums in large cities, and low wages soon drew the attention of a number of socially conscious people nationwide including Jane Addams, who founded the world-famous Hull House settlement in Chicago in 1889. Seeking a country place where she could bring underprivileged women and their children in the summer, she traveled to Waukegan with her benefactor, Louise DeKoven Bowen. Mayor Fred Buck met them at the depot and drove them to view property he owned north of town—property which the city council had turned down when Buck proposed it for a park. As the sleigh reached the crest of the hill at Sheridan Road and Greenwood Avenue on that snowy November day in 1910, the women knew they had found what they were looking for with one glance at the glistening panorama of slopes, hills, and ravines.

Facing page: Robert M. Ingalls and R.J. Douglas volunteered for duty in the Illinois Navy Reserves, 4th Division, at the time of the Spanish-American War in 1898. They were assigned to the battleship Oregon, which fought in the battle off Santiago. Courtesy, Lake County Museum

Below: At the turn of the century, winter snows didn't put a damper on Libertyville's Market Day, held the third Wednesday of each month. Horse-drawn sleighs and wagons converged on Milwaukee Avenue, causing traffic problems much like the scene today when Libertyville holds Market Day every Thursday during the summer and early fall on the same avenue. Courtesy, Libertyville-Mundelein Historical Society

Above: *Libertyville civic leaders convinced officials of the Chicago, Milwaukee & St. Paul Railroad to run a daily train between the town and Chicago. Villagers provided the depot at the foot of Sprague Street (East Cook Avenue) and provided the land, labor, material, and funds. The first steam locomotive arrived in May 1880. The depot was moved to the west side of Milwaukee Avenue, north of Lake Avenue. Courtesy, Libertyville-Mundelein Historical Society*

Right: *"Premiums have always been paid in full," reads the publicity on the one-half-mile racetrack at the Lake County Fair Grounds in Libertyville. The Lake County Agricultural Society was organized in 1852 and held 44 successive fairs. The grounds boasted a "large main hall for exhibits, comodious [sic] amphitheater, dining halls and abundance of good stalls for accommodation of stock." The grounds subsequently became a gravel pit, and were then transformed into today's Lake Minear. Courtesy, Libertyville-Mundelein Historical Society*

Above: *Music at the early Lake County fairs was provided by the Libertyville village band, a group of about two dozen musicians. The fair was held in Libertyville for about 75 years, until the property was sold in the 1920s for gravel mining operations; the site is now Lake Minear. Courtesy, Libertyville-Mundelein Historical Society*

Above: *In 1905 F.W. Foulds outgrew its factory in Cincinnati and moved operations closer to its largest market, Chicago, by purchasing the National Macaroni Company in Libertyville. Dropping its milling operation, the company turned to full production of macaroni products. Sold in 1923 to the Grocery Store Products Company, it was purchased some 50 years later and is now Foulds, Inc. Its macaroni, spaghetti, and egg noodle products are sold nationwide, and Foulds also produces macaroni for Kraft Inc. at its same Libertyville plant at 520 E. Church Street. Courtesy, Libertyville-Mundelein Historical Society*

Right: *Local farmers were able to deliver their milk at a "drive-thru" window of the Lake Zurich Creamery in the early 1900s. Run by James Davidson and managed by Fergie Harkness, the Creamery had a drive-up window with a ledge on which farmers put their milk. Kerosene lanterns strung on wires lit the way on dark mornings. The Creamery was converted into the Mionske Apartments in 1965. Courtesy, Lake County Museum*

The only house on the property was the former country home of John Charles Haines, mayor of Chicago in 1878. Mess halls and dormitories were built for the summer campers—who once included a teenage Benny Goodman—and the 72-acre site was christened Bowen Country Club. It served the poor of Chicago until 1963, when it was sold to the Waukegan Park District. Ten years later the Haines House was leased to the Waukegan Historical Society for its headquarters.

Captain Edward Bradley, a Princeton graduate from Philadelphia, began to help homeless and neglected boys in a store in Chicago in 1884. He also wanted to get them out of the city into the fresh air, and brought them to camp on Cedar Lake in Lake Villa. In 1887 he purchased a quarter section of land and established a year-round home known as Allendale Farm.

With its strong Methodist roots, Lake Bluff was attractive to the officials of the Chicago Deaconesses Home for Orphans, and in 1894 they rented a small house in the village for six children. According to historian Elmer Vliet, the project was incorporated as the Lake Bluff Methodist Deaconesses Orphanage, and a year later a larger building was erected to accommodate 30 children. By 1900 the facility had to be enlarged again. Before it was closed in 1979, thousands of youngsters passed under the care of the director, Deaconess Lucy Judson, and her successors.

Temperance as an issue is a recurring theme in the history of the area. On November 25, 1905, a group met in Lake Forest to protest the liquor, gambling, and vice that apparently was running rampant in Highwood. They soon joined forces with a like-minded group from Highland Park and concerned citizens of Highwood, and became known as the Law and Order League. Proceedings were promptly brought against almost all 12 saloons in Highwood, but fines did not deter the tavern owners. Finally in May 1907 the league was successful in pushing a law through the Illinois legislature forbidding the sale, distribution, or gift of intoxicating liquors within 1 ⅛ miles of a U.S. naval training school or a U.S. military post. The deadline for compliance was January 1, 1908. This effectively put out of business all saloon owners in Highwood, and those south of 14th Street in North Chicago.

The Saloon Act of 1907 further provided that by popular vote people of a township could decide if they wanted to prohibit the sale and licensing of liquor. At elections in the spring of 1908, Benton, Newport, and Warren townships voted to ban saloons. Shields, Fremont, and East Deerfield (West Deerfield had become a separate township in 1887) did not have any saloons; and in Grant, Wauconda, Cuba, and Ela no petitions for election were filed. It is reported that in Grant, where sum-

mer resorts abounded, not one person could be found who would circulate a petition. Antioch, Avon, Waukegan, Libertyville, Vernon, and West Deerfield all voted wet.

An interesting sidelight is that Winthrop Harbor voted to remain wet but the state supreme court ruled against them, ordering them to follow the rest of Benton Township.

In an era that saw the invention of the telephone (1876) and the light bulb (1879), the first flight with a gas-powered engine (1903), and the production of the first Model A's (1903), Lake County had its own inventors. Edward Amet, working in his laboratory at the Chicago Recording and Scale Works on Waukegan's lakefront, developed the magniscope, which projected moving pictures on a screen. Up to that time film could only be viewed by one person at a time using a peepshow device, Thomas Edison's kinetoscope. In 1894 Amet demonstrated his invention (examples of which can be found at the Museum of Science and Industry in Chicago and in the Smithsonian Institution collection) for George Spoor, who managed the Phoenix Opera House in Waukegan. For several years the two men collaborated on the making and showing of moving pictures to audiences in the area.

Waukeganites were the actors in those first movies, including a women's boxing match and a re-creation of the Battle of Manila filmed at Druce and Third lakes.

Spoor went on to cofound the Essanay Film Company in Chicago with other partners. Amet, who was more interested in science than business, continued to invent. Among his patents are an automatic weighing and recording scale for railroad cars, and the "nickel-in-the-slot" weighing machines for humans.

Elisha Gray, a civic leader and trustee of the Presbyterian church in Highland Park, is said to have invented and demonstrated a telephone to an astounded crowd at the church on December 28, 1874—two years before Alexander Graham Bell filed for a patent for his telephone. Local stories relate that Gray filed within hours of Bell.

While the county had been growing and stretching, events in Europe had catapulted most of the western world into war. The

Above: *Waukegan Mayor Fred W. Buck, who served a two-year term from 1909 to 1911, was one of nine children of a German-born butcher and his wife. He was educated in Waukegan and opened his own meat shop on North Genesee Street. Buck is probably best remembered as the owner of property north of town that he showed to Jane Addams and Louise Bowen in 1911. The property was site of the Haines Farmhouse, and under Addams' direction it became a summer retreat for underprivileged youth known as Bowen Country Club. Courtesy, Waukegan Historical Society*

Above: *The Lake Bluff Children's Home dates back to 1894, when a small house in the village became home to six children. The Lake Bluff Methodist Deaconesses Orphanage saw numerous expansions during its 85-year history, and cared for thousands of parentless youngsters. Courtesy,* Waukegan News-Sun

United States finally was drawn into the conflict on April 6, 1917. It was the Great War, the World War, and the war to end all wars. Of course, no one knew at the time that it was only World War I.

The community reacted immediately. Frank Knaak, a Waukegan wireless operator, was the first to enlist in the Navy. Twenty employees of the wire mill enlisted in the first days. The guard at Great Lakes Naval Training Station was doubled. Voliva, according to the *Daily Sun,* banned all festivities in Zion saying, "The situation is too serious for fri-

volity and pleasure." Waukegan police chief Thomas Tyrell, who in 1914 had threatened to arrest any woman who appeared on the street in a slit skirt, posted a special guard at the water works and the wire mill.

Major A.V. Smith mobilized Battery C of the First Illinois National Guard—which had been organized in Waukegan in 1902—and they left Lake County almost immediately. In Libertyville 1,200 people turned out to hear the Navy band, and speakers drumming up enlistments for the Navy. On the down side, the front-page headlines of news-

Waukegan—the Motion Picture Capital of the World. It might have been, as resident Edward H. Amet is credited with inventing, in 1894, the first practical motion picture projector, the Amet Magniscope, said to be an improvement over Thomas Edison's kinctoscope. Amet manufactured about 500 of this second model, shown here, in 1894-1895. Photo by The Smithsonian Institution. Courtesy E.W. Plonien Collection, Waukegan Historical Society

Right: *First Lieutenant Homer Walston Dahringer of Waukegan, a popular high school and college basketball star, was one of the area's first World War I Heroes. Dahringer, who served in the First Aero Squadron, was shot down over enemy lines in 1918 and his body returned for burial in 1921. Waukegan's American Legion post, founded in 1919, was named for Dahringer. Courtesy, Waukegan Historical Society*

papers constantly blasted the "slackers" who were rushing to get marriage licenses in order to be exempt from military service.

Word was received that G.S. Porre of Highwood, who was serving with a Canadian contingent in France, was the first Lake County soldier to die after the United States entered the war.

Local industry geared up for the war effort, and the Winthrop Harbor Truck Company received an order for 235 "auto-trucks." According to the *Daily Sun,* "Winthrop Harbor promises to be a big automobile manufacturing center in the near future." Originally called Spring Bluff, Winthrop Harbor had taken its name from an early boat-building firm and in the early 1900s boasted several industries.

Funds for Waukegan harbor improvements, an uphill battle from day one, were finally allotted in the amount of $100,000 as part of the war effort.

A holiday was declared on June 5, 1917, to allow men between the ages of 21 and 31 to register for the draft. The day was marked with a parade of 5,000 "sons and daughters of liberty," leading from the Waukegan court-

house to Foss Park in North Chicago. The following day the *Daily Sun* reported: "With a rush that swept the registrars off their feet, young men swarmed down to the polling places to list their names." All told, 6,238 registered in Lake County. Of that number, 632 were called in the first draft in July.

Lake County went over the top in the third Liberty Loan drive in the spring of 1918. Given a goal of $2.4 million, they sold $2.5 million in a one-month period marked by rallies, band concerts, and a county-wide tour by the popular Hollywood star Douglas Fairbanks. In Waukegan 10,000 people lined the streets to watch draftees being escorted to the train station by parading Liberty Loan promoters.

Everyone on the homefront rallied to support the war effort. In Highland Park, when it was discovered that a young soldier from Fort Sheridan had attended church three times in one day because there was nothing else to do, women opened an Army-Navy center. According to *Pioneer to Commuter* by Marvyn Wittelle, the center provided "magazines, newspapers, a phonograph or some other giddy, merry-making device . . ." This effort was soon proclaimed "the first of its type in the U.S." by government inspectors, and was the forerunner of the United Service Organization of World War II.

Lake County farmers, according to Jane Snodgrass Johnson's *History of Lake County,* produced 1.8 million bushels of wheat in 1918 in response to the government's request for 600,000.

Lake Bluff, a village of 700, was cited by the Red Cross for contributing more generously in proportion to its size than any other community in the state.

At the same time, the county had to cope with domestic problems. A million-dollar fire destroyed the Manufacturers Terminal in Waukegan, a group of factory buildings including a government warehouse for war supplies. The federal government demanded fire-safety improvements in the city if they were to continue to do business there.

Then, in the waning months of the war, the dreaded Spanish Influenza struck military personnel and civilians alike. On September 23, 1918, according to the *Daily Sun,* there were 4,500 cases of the pneumonia-like disease at Great Lakes Naval Station alone. A day later that figure was doubled, and it was announced that 200 had died at the base. Schools, churches, and theaters were closed. Emergency hospitals staffed by the Red Cross were set up at Bowen Country Club and a vacant building on 11th Street in North Chicago. Captain William Moffett, commander of the naval training station, loaned the city four Navy nurses. The epidemic was blamed on the shortage of doctors; a shortage of coal which led to cold, damp homes; and a lack of drugs. Every day the paper carried stories of new fatalities, often two or three in a single family. October 6, 1918, was described as "Black Sunday" in Waukegan. There were eight burials in Oakwood Cemetery that day, and orders were given to dig 12 graves for the next day. Johnson claimed that 2,800 civilians in Lake County were stricken with influenza in the one-month period.

Further, Johnson stated, some 4,200 Lake County residents served in the armed forces in World War I. Typical of the men who went to war and were lionized by the public was Homer W. Dahringer, popular basketball star of Waukegan High School and the University of Illinois. He enlisted in the first days of the war and was commissioned an officer in the First Aero Squadron—a dashing assignment in a war that people tended to paint glamorous.

When Dahringer was shot down over enemy lines on September 17, 1918, the newspaper said, " . . . he has joined the big band of heroes who gave their lives that Prussianism should not survive." The American Legion Post, formed in Waukegan in 1919, was named for Dahringer. When his body was brought home for burial in 1921, legionnaires walked to the cemetery beside a horse-drawn gun carriage on which the casket was borne.

Ruth Besley, Dahringer's fiancee and a descendant of the Besley Brewery family, did not marry until 1977 when she was 86 years old.

"Waukegan Runs Riot With Joy," screamed the headline in the *Daily Sun* on November 11, 1918, marking the signing of the armistice to end the war. The news came at 2:30 A.M., and the wire-mill whistle blew almost immediately. Despite the hour people poured into the streets, blowing whistles, ringing bells, and building bonfires. That day factories were shut down, school was called off, and storekeepers locked their doors. Everyone in Waukegan was urged to join in a victory parade. Thousands across the county participated in what the *Daily Sun* called the "wildest celebration in history."

Left: *When the wire-mill whistle blew at 2:30 the morning of November 11, 1918, Waukegan didn't stop to ask what happened. Hundreds of people went out into the streets to celebrate the end of the "war to end all wars." Factories shut down, schools closed, and thousands of people joined in the victory celebrations. "Welcome home" parades, like this one, marked the town's delight at having its young men home from abroad, the war won. Photo by R.L. Blakemore. Courtesy, Waukegan Historical Society*

Right: *Nearly a quarter of a million visitors had to be transported in and out of Mundelein for the closing exercises of the 28th International Eucharistic Congress of the Catholic Church, held in Chicago in June 1926. Cardinal George Mundelein used the occasion to show off his new seminary in Mundelein. Courtesy, Libertyville-Mundelein Historical Society*

CHAPTER 4

EBB AND FLOW

Lake County went roaring into the 1920s along with the rest of the nation. Fast cars and fast dances, illegal booze and gangsters, and shifting populations and shifty politicians became the hallmarks of the era.

Chicago and Lake County were connected for the first time by a concrete highway which came up Waukegan Road to Route 176 and branched east to Green Bay Road and north into North Chicago.

Forsaking tradition, a young couple chose the lotus beds of Grass Lake for their wedding. The newspaper reported that the lotus grew higher than the heads of people standing in the boats.

The first large migration of blacks occurred after World War I, due to the increased need for laborers in northern industries. According to James Dorsey, writing in *Up South*, 73 percent of blacks were in rural areas in 1910 and by 1960 had shifted so that 73 percent were in urban areas. In Waukegan prior to 1910 blacks lived throughout the city. Following World War I they began to concentrate in sections of the south and west sides of the city.

In November of 1920, 103-year-old Deliah King of Zion exercised the right to vote granted to women by the 19th Amendment on August 26, 1920. She went to the polls in the snow to vote for Warren Harding for president.

That same election brought into the state's attorney's office A.V. Smith, the World War I hero who led the National Guard to battle. He soon became known as a fearless enemy of Prohibition violators. His raiders, dubbed "the sponge squad," were a force to be reckoned with, striking at stills in private homes, searching out blind pigs, and raiding speakeasies at the lake resorts.

Within days after Prohibition became effective on January 16, 1920, the *Waukegan Daily Gazette* announced the first raid in the

city of Waukegan. A still in a private residence had been discovered, "dropping out raisin whiskey as deadly as you can imagine." When it was learned that grocery stores in Lake Forest were sold out of raisins, police traced the customers to two estates where they found stills being operated by servants.

The *Antioch News* headlined: "Chase beer runners through Antioch at a 60 mile clip."

It was no secret that booze continued to flow throughout the county, but now it was controlled by gangsters. The *Chicago Tribune,* on September 2, 1932, alleged that "[George 'Bugs'] Moran, according to underworld gossip commands the vice, slot machine and booze rackets in Lake County." It was a well-known fact that Moran hung out at Leo Mongoven's resort on Bluff Lake. Meanwhile, hearsay had it that Al Capone's cohorts adopted the Mineola Hotel on Fox Lake as their rest and relaxation haven.

In the pre-dawn hours of June 1, 1930,

mobsters from both gangs were gunned down on the porch of Manning's resort in Fox Lake as they dined together. Police were at a loss as to why they were together and who had done the shooting, which came to be known as the Fox Lake Massacre.

Although it was business as usual most of the time, the covert operations necessarily led to some changes. Until Prohibition, for example, Fox Lake residents paid no property taxes as the entire tax burden was carried by the resorts and hotels.

Young people continued to be lured to the lakes, where three huge dance halls were built in the Antioch area alone. All three eventually were destroyed by fire. Built first, in 1918, the Channel Lake Pavilion lasted until 1951. The Channel Lake Pavilion on the Lake, built in 1923 and burned in 1933, boasted a bowling alley as well as a dance floor. Grandest of all was the Antioch Palace, billed as the "wonder amusement place." It opened with a grand ball on April 28, 1927, following what the *Antioch News* described as a boom year for Antioch. The Palace, which sported a 125-by-180-foot dance floor, only lasted until 1932.

In Waukegan couples roller skated and participated in walk-a-thons during the 1930s, and jitterbugged to the big band sounds of the 1940s in the Rink. Built in the early 1930s, the building houses a shooting gallery today.

Governor Len Small, who during his campaign for office pledged to lift Illinois out of the mud and who twice set the national record for paving highways, was elected on the Republican ticket in 1920. Two years later he was on trial at the Lake County courthouse in Waukegan before Judge Clair C. Edwards, accused of fraud and embezzlement of state funds while he was state treasurer.

Before the trial even got under way on May 11, 1922, Lake County officials were haggling with their counterparts in Sangamon County, demanding immediate payment of the cost of the trial. Sangamon officials replied indignantly that they would pay in their own good time, and eventually a settlement was reached.

The trial dragged on for more than a month, with the *Waukegan Daily News* reporting at one point, "More dry stuff in Small trial." Finally, on June 24, the governor was found not guilty by a jury of his peers, which included a steel mill employee, taxi driver, fireman, and bricklayer.

It was a popular verdict, according to the newspaper, but there was a sad footnote. Two days later, his wife was dead following a stroke. The paper said it was from "overjoy."

Mansion building on the North Shore, which began in the early part of the century when it became fashionable for the wealthy to have a town house and a country home, went into high gear in the heady postwar years. Architect David Adler became the darling of the monied class. Born in Milwaukee and educated in Europe, Adler's career was launched with the Glencoe home he designed for his uncle. His work ranged from Massachusetts to Hawaii, but in Lake County was done mostly in Lake Forest and Lake Bluff and included the 47-room Lester Armour house, which in 1978 was the setting for the movie, *The Wedding.*

For his own use Adler remodeled a farmhouse in Libertyville, retaining its original simplicity while adding gardens, a courtyard, and a Normandy tower. The estate—now known as Adler Park—is owned by the Village of Libertyville and the house is leased to the David Adler Cultural Center.

Adler flourished from 1912 to 1935, when he was injured in a fall during the Mill Creek Hunt in Wadsworth. Richard Pratt, author of *David Adler: The Architect and His Work,* quotes him as saying, "My work is all in the period of the great house which today, alas, is over."

Another significant Lake Forest architect was Howard Van Doren Shaw, who built a summer home in the city in 1897. He designed a number of mansions but is best remembered for Market Square in Lake Forest, which has been termed the first planned shopping center in the country. The project was born when an association, formed in 1912 to buy up and replace the wooden, run-down buildings in the center of town, hired Shaw to renovate the area. Shaw's brick buildings, trimmed with stucco and limestone, give Market Square its character reminiscent of an English market town. It boasts two towers: one with a clock, the other with a sundial. Slate roofs, balconies, and a fountain dedicated to Shaw accent what is still a busy retail center today.

Many of the great estates, which also included vast farms along Green Bay Road, were subdivided beginning in the 1930s. The Medill Patterson estate is now the setting for Hawthorn Shopping Center in Vernon Hills; the Philip D. Armour II mansion houses United Educators, with the surrounding property given over to residential development; Lake Forest Academy-Ferry Hall bought the J. Ogden Armour property and maintains the palatial mansion and formal gardens; and the Samuel Insull estate on Milwaukee Avenue in Libertyville, which was later bought by John Cuneo, is currently being considered for development.

Samuel Insull is a story unto himself. Born in England, he came to the United States as Thomas Edison's private secretary and soon began taking over small electric companies, which he organized into a holding company,

Facing page: *Fox Lake's Mineola Hotel has a checkered history. Perhaps the doyenne of the resort community's hotels, the Mineola was reportedly the hangout of mobster Al Capone. George "Bugs" Moran's gang made a nearby Bluff Lake resort their headquarters. The 1930 "Fox Lake Massacre" saw members of both gangs gunned down on the porch of another Fox Lake resort. The Mineola is being restored by its owners. Courtesy,* Waukegan News-Sun

Middle West Utilities Co. In Lake County he connected villages with a generating plant and offered service to farms, earning himself the title "father of rural electrification."

Insull controlled the Public Service Company of Northern Illinois and Peoples Gas Light and Coke Company. According to Robert P. Howard, by the late 1920s Insull's utilities produced one-eighth of the nation's electricity and gas, and served more than 4 million customers. Because the electric interurban railroads were his customers, he also acquired them. Insull's personal fortune was estimated at $150 million.

Complex financial maneuvering, the revelation that politicians into whose campaigns he had poured millions of dollars were allowed to buy stock at half price, and the stockmarket crash of 1929 brought Insull's empire tumbling down. In 1932 Insull's hold-

Above and right: *Liberty-ville architect David Adler, described as "the last of the great eclectic architects," designed at least 50 and built 43 of "the great houses." Many of his homes were done in nearby Lake Forest and Lake Bluff for such well-to-do families as the Fields, Dicks, Cudahys, Armours, McCormicks, Ryersons, and Florsheims. His remodeled farmhouse in Liberty-ville included a courtyard decorated with a Normandy tower. Courtesy, Libertyville-Mundelein Historical Society*

ing company went into receivership and thousands of small investors lost their money. He fled to Greece, was extradited, and was prosecuted in federal court but acquitted on the grounds that holding companies were not subject to regulation. He died in Paris in 1938 at the age of 79.

Cardinal George Mundelein also had his eye on Lake County, and in 1921 he decided to relocate the major seminary of the Catholic Archdiocese of Chicago to a settlement west of Libertyville then known as Area. Its very first name was Mechanics Grove, because the early arrivals were millwrights and carpenters. Then along came John Holcomb, who in 1885 donated land for the Wisconsin Central Railroad (predecessor of the Soo line), and grateful residents renamed the village for him.

The name Rockefeller was taken briefly when the villagers entertained the pie-in-the-

Above and left: When architect David Adler remodeled his own farmhouse in Libertyville, he kept the simplicity while adding gardens and his own unique touches. At left is the dining porch, above the dressing room. Adler's house is owned by the Village of Libertyville and is leased to the David Adler Cultural Center. Courtesty, Libertyville-Mundelein Historical Society

Above: *This gazebo at the David Adler Cultural Center was burned, apparently by vandals, in 1979. A replica welcomes visitors to Libertyville's Heritage Area from the entrance of Central Park on Milwaukee Avenue near the downtown district. It was built by the village and dedicated in June 1980. Courtesy, Libertyville-Mundelein Historical Society*

sky idea that William Rockefeller, a stockholder in the railroad, would be their benefactor. It is said he rode in on the inaugural run, got off and looked around, and got back on, never to be heard from again. This, of course, prompted yet another name change.

Arthur Sheldon then ran a business school, which was way ahead of its time in offering women employment. The acronym of his motto—Ability, Reliability, Endurance and Action—was adopted as the next name. When Sheldon declared bankruptcy, Cardinal Mundelein bought his property which included Mud Lake.

Not one to stint, the cardinal built 14 classical Georgian buildings and formal gardens on the beautiful, wooded grounds surrounding the lake, which he renamed St. Mary. The University of St. Mary of the Lake's Feehan Memorial Library, which contains thousands of rare books, is recognized as one of the outstanding libraries in the country in the fields of patristics and church history.

It seemed only fitting to residents that, with such a beautiful university in their midst, they once more rename their community. It has been Mundelein ever since.

When the 28th International Eucharistic Congress of the Catholic Church was held in Chicago in June 1926, Cardinal Mundelein, anxious to show off his new university, hosted the closing exercises there on Sunday, June 24. The movement of people in and out of the small town is considered one of the feats of modern transportation. According to William D. Middleton's *North Shore, America's Fastest Interurban,* it was the greatest mass movement in interurban history without a single mishap or injury. In the 18 hours from daybreak to midnight, 820 trains (5,216 cars) had moved 225,000 people into the town of Mundelein and 275,000 out. Thousands more were moved on the Soo line, the Milwaukee Road, and the North Western.

Attracted by a skilled labor force, good rail transportation, and its proximity to Chicago, new industry also moved into Lake County during this period. Johns-Manville, an established company whose products have included roofing material, rock-wool insulation, and corrugated siding, bought 255 acres of then unincorporated swampland on the Waukegan lakefront in 1919. Its first building, completed in 1923, contained 28 acres of floor space. The Waukegan plant at one time was the second largest of the corporation's 106 plants, consisting of 12 buildings and employing more than 1,000 with a payroll of over $15 million.

Abbott Laboratories, now one of the largest private-industry employers in the county, established its roots here in 1920. Dr. Wallace C. Abbott plowed the first furrow for a new building in North Chicago, then hosted a picnic to celebrate. The physician and pharmacist had started his company in the kitchen of his Ravenswood home in 1891. The demand for domestically made drugs during World War I caused rapid expansion and the move north.

By Thanksgiving Day 1925, Abbott's entire operation was in place in North Chicago. Since then it has grown to include more than 2 million feet of floor space on the original site, as well as a complex of buildings in an unincorporated area southwest of North Chicago.

Thousands of children were familiar with the Abbott logo during the 1930s when they were given daily dosages of Haliver Oil, a nutritional supplement. Scores of those same children, "gone to soldiers" during World War II, were saved by the blood plasma Abbott produced in North Chicago.

Johnson Motors got its start with the first homemade marine-engine crafted by the Johnson brothers in their father's blacksmith shop in Terre Haute, Indiana. They branched off for a time, making motors for bicycles and calling themselves the Johnson Motor Wheel Company of Terre Haute. After moving to South Bend, Indiana, they began producing outboard motors in 1921. Needing a place to test their new product, they then moved the operation to a 114-acre site on the Waukegan lakefront.

Johnson Motors became a division of the newly formed Outboard Marine Corporation in 1936, and by 1975 the company employed 3,600 people and had a payroll of $48 million. During World War II they manufactured landing craft for the Navy, and then retooled for the recreation boom that followed.

Not all of the development was on the lakefront. In Barrington, which had been incorporated in 1865 as a rural market center, Jewel Tea Company built a manufacturing plant on 211 acres in 1930. The beautifully landscaped, modern facility was way ahead of its time, providing amenities such as bowling alleys and tennis courts for workers. Known as the Park Corporation since 1985 when it separated from Jewel Food Stores, the company is still a food-service and retail supplier of desserts, coffee, tea, and other beverages.

With industrialization also came the struggle by laborers to organize. In the fall of 1919 striking wire mill workers held weekly meetings, usually at the Slovenic Hall on 10th Street in Waukegan. On November 10 they were addressed by Mayor Daniel Hoan, re-

Below: The imposing J. Ogden Armour estate, Mellody Farm, was purchased by trustees of the Lake Forest Academy after the school was severely damaged by fire in 1946. Founded in 1856 by the Lake Forest Association, the boys' preparatory school was one of a triad invisioned by the group. The girl's seminary, Ferry Hall, opened in 1869 and merged with the Academy in 1974. Lake Forest College, the third member of the group, opened in 1876. Courtesy, Waukegan Historical Society

ferred to in the *Waukegan Daily Sun* as the "socialist mayor of Milwaukee." Waukegan mayor Julius Bidinger promptly issued a proclamation forbidding any more meetings which would "incite feelings of striking wire mill men." Two days later the strikers defied his order, and since they outnumbered the police by a ratio of 60-to-1, no action was taken.

The American Legion took up the cause, and marched to 10th Street on November 23, 1919, to stop the next meeting. When confronted with a larger group, the union men simply moved across the street and continued their meeting in a hall in North Chicago. They were led by Nick Keller, who later served as Waukegan city commissioner and in the Illinois State Legislature.

The year 1937 saw labor unrest all across the country, and the sitdown strike staged by Fansteel employees gained national attention. On February 17, 1937, at 3:30 P.M., 100 workers ejected foremen and other management personnel from two of the buildings, and took control of the premises in an attempt to get management to recognize their right to organize under the Congress of Industrial Organizations (CIO).

Circuit Judge Ralph Dady promptly issued an injunction against them but Sheriff Lawrence Doolittle hesitated to enforce it, fearing loss of life. For nine days the strikers held out under adverse conditions, including extreme cold and hunger, while police as well as supporters gathered around the plant. Finally, on February 26, the sheriff rousted the strikers with tear gas and was commended for ending a difficult situation without loss of life. It had been hoped throughout the strike that a peaceful solution would be reached, with Martin Durkin, state director of labor, urging both sides to negotiate. But Fansteel vice president and general manager, Robert J. Aitchison, refused to sit down with CIO representatives.

Of the 100 original strikers, 59 returned to their jobs. Thirty-seven were fired and the case, according to Jon R. Tennyson, went all the way to the Supreme Court which ruled in 1939 that sitdown strikes constituted an illegal seizure of buildings. Labor Secretary Frances Perkins called 1937 the most savage year in the history of twentieth-century labor, but by the end of the year 8 million workers were carrying union cards.

Two notorious crimes also brought Lake County into the national headlines. Rondout, an important rail junction at the turn of the century, was the scene of a daring train robbery on June 12, 1924. Two members of a gang rode a Milwaukee Road mail-train carrying payroll money from Chicago and forced the engineer to stop just north of Rondout, where

Right: In 1921 Cardinal George Mundelein began construction of the University of St. Mary of the Lake, the major seminary of the Catholic Archdiocese of Chicago. He purchased land that had belonged to Arthur Sheldon's business school and Sheldonhurst Farm, including Mud Lake. The cardinal built 14 classical Georgian buildings and formal gardens on the grounds surrounding the lake, renamed St. Mary. The town was eventually renamed Mundelein in his honor. Courtesy, Libertyville-Mundelein Historical Society

the rest of the gang were waiting. Using tear gas, they rousted out the crew and carried off sacks of money. One of the gang was accidentally shot by another at the scene and, although they sped away in two stolen Cadillacs, the accident eventually led to their capture. As a result, two masterminds were implicated: William Fahy, a respected railroad investigator; and a two-bit Chicago politician. It was the largest railroad heist—$3 million—until the Great British Train Robbery in 1963. One million dollars has never been found.

The second notorious crime remains an unsolved mystery. Nude and severely burned, 29-year-old Elfreda Knaak was found on the morning of October 30, 1928, in the furnace room of the locked Lake Bluff Village Hall. She died two days later and although a coroner's jury decided she had burned herself, doctors attending her declared that impossible.

The case has never been closed.

Health care greatly expanded during the 1920s, with the opening in Waukegan of Victory Memorial Hospital in 1922 to replace Jane McAlister Hospital; St. Therese Hospital in 1929; and Condell Memorial Hospital in Libertyville in 1928. Lake County General Hospital (opened in 1915 for the indigent) and Highland Park Hospital (opened in 1918) were already in operation. Lake Forest had the Alice Home, built in 1899 on the campus of Lake Forest College, to care for its medical needs. In 1941 Lake Forest Hospital was built, replacing the Alice Home as the city's major medical facility.

The entire country had entered the decade of the 1930s broke and bitter, and in 1932 people looked to Franklin D. Roosevelt to put their "feet on the sunny side of the street" once again.

Above: Arthur Sheldon ran a business school in present-day Mundelein that was rather ahead of its time, offering employment for women. His motto, "Ability, Reliability, Endurance, and Action" (AREA) gave the town its fourth name (previously it had been Mechanics Grove, Holcomb, and Rockefeller). Sheldon's school eventually went bankrupt and the land he owned in Area was purchased by Cardinal George Mundelein, who gave the village its present name. Courtesy, Libertyville-Mundelein Historical Society

Above: *According to William D. Middleton's North Shore, America's Fastest Interurban, 820 trains containing 5,216 cars moved some 225,000 people into Mundelein and 275,000 out during an 18-hour period on June 24, 1926. The crowd was attending the 28th International Eucharistic Congress closing ceremonies on the grounds of St. Mary of the Lake Seminary, in Mundelein. Courtesy, Libertyville-Mundelein Historical Society*

Although it was a landslide victory across the country for Roosevelt as well as Democratic candidates for Congress and state government, the headline in *The Waukegan News-Sun* on November 9, 1932, read: "G.O.P. County Slate Winner." True to its Republican tradition, the county cast 23,994 votes for Hoover compared to 21,139 for Roosevelt. Only Antioch, Grant, Waukegan, Libertyville, Wauconda, and Vernon townships gave Roosevelt a majority.

Roosevelt was inaugurated on March 4, 1933, and called for a four-day banking moratorium, although banks in more than 20 states, including Illinois, had already closed as a result of the Depression. Locally, Abbott Laboratories and the Chicago Hardware Foundry were forced to make payments with scrip because their money was inaccessible. The Waukegan-North Chicago Chamber of Commerce met to discuss ways to deal with the situation. On March 7, banks were allowed to deal in emergency funds. By March 15, banks in Antioch, Barrington, Lake Forest, Fox Lake, Grayslake, and Lake Villa were open for business as usual. The First National Bank of Waukegan did not reopen until July 17, and reported that business was mild that day.

Agriculture was still an important factor in the economy of Lake County at that time. Although farmers from surrounding counties staged a milk strike in May 1933, the 860 dairy farmers of the Lake County Pure Milk Association voted to continue to send their milk to market on the basis of a promised rate increase. Local dairies soon raised the price of milk to 10 cents a quart, giving the farmers $1.75 per 100 pounds, an increase of 30 cents, according to *The Waukegan News-Sun*. Several years later, however, Lake County dairymen found it necessary to participate in a short-term milk strike to gain another increase.

Almost immediately after taking office, Roosevelt launched a series of federal programs to aid the depressed economy. Many of these had a lasting impact on Lake County communities.

The Civilian Conservation Corps (CCC) was a program designed to put young, unemployed men to work in army-like camps, working on reforesting, soil erosion, and flood control. One of the CCC camps was on the site of the present Chain O'Lakes State Park, which is intersected by the Fox River and borders Grass, Marie, and Bluff lakes. The site was designated a Conservation Area during the CCC days, was purchased by the state in 1945, and became a state park in 1957.

Under the Civil Works Administration (CWA), the Works Project Administration (WPA), and the Public Works Administration (PWA)—which were established to provide jobs while aiding communities in public projects—bridges were built over ravines in Lake Bluff, sea walls were erected in Fox Lake, a school was added onto in Winthrop Harbor, and parks were improved in Waukegan.

It is recorded that local governments also tightened their belts. The mayor of Waukegan, Peter W. Petersen, had his salary reduced from $3,700 to $3,000 in 1933. George Hollister, president of Fox Lake from 1929 to 1935, reduced the village's bonded debt from $28,000 to $8,000. When the newly formed Progressive Party took office in Lake Bluff in 1929, the village was in debt to the tune of $66,000. By 1937 it had a balance on hand of $5,548 and its bonded indebtedness was reduced to $26,000.

During the Depression many people who owned summer cottages in Lake County—and who were either out of work or unable to afford the rents in Chicago—began to live at the lakes year-round. By 1936 there were enough year-round residents in Round Lake Beach, a subdivision of Round Lake which had been promoted by L.B. Harris as a summer enclave in 1930, for it to become incorporated. (Round Lake Park was incorporated in 1947 and Round Lake Heights in 1957.)

Neighbor helped neighbor in those stark times and many instances of personal charity are recorded, some of which had a long-term effect. Walking along Market Street in Waukegan, which had become a poverty-stricken black ghetto, Anna Perry Thomas was appalled to see young children locked inside their houses, alone all day. Their parents were obliged to take whatever jobs they could find and had no one with whom to leave the children.

On June 17, 1934, Thomas opened a nursery school for 17 children in the home of her sister, Bertha Perry, on Utica Street in Waukegan. "Sixteen of those children had something wrong with them," she said. They suffered everything from malnutrition to bowed bones to just plain weariness.

Almost from the start the nursery school attracted the attention of philanthropic citizens, and when Thomas was asked what she did if a parent could not pay the meager tuition, she replied, "Ask the Presbyterians and the Methodists, the Kiwanians and the Rotarians and others." Long before day-care centers came into popular vogue, Thomas' Happy Day Nursery continued to expand.

In 1975 Joseph Staver, retired vice president of the Chicago Title and Trust Company, spearheaded a successful community drive to build a new school on McAlister Avenue land

Below: *Not a single mishap or injury was recorded by the Chicago North Shore and Milwaukee Railroad in transporting a quarter of a million people into and out of Mundelein during the 28th International Eucharistic Congress in June 1926. Thousands of visitors were transported on the Soo Line, the Milwaukee Road, and the North Western railroad trains as well. Courtesy, Libertyville-Mundelein Historical Society*

Left: *Workers at Johnson Motors in Waukegan put the final touches on Sea Horse Outboard Motors before shipment. Johnson Motors began producing outboard motors in 1921, and, needing a place to test their product, moved to a 114-acre site on Waukegan's lakefront. Johnson became a division of Outboard Marine Corp. in 1936, and produced landing craft for the U.S. Navy during World War II. Photo by Harold G. Mason. Courtesy, Waukegan Historical Society*

which they frequently referred to "the boss." It was Frank Just they were talking about.

F. Ward Just succeeded his father and also was a staunch Republican but, unlike Frank, occasionally endorsed a Democrat because he believed in the two-party system. When he died in 1970, Governor Richard Ogilvie called him "a tower of strength in the state and the community." The mantle was passed on to his son, Ward S. Just, who by that time was established as a Washington, D.C., journalist and whose political leanings were more liberal. The era of Just-dominated Republican politics had passed. However, young Ward immortalized it in a fictionalized account, *Family Trust.*

Another who helped shape the face of the county was Dr. W.C. Petty, county su-

Above: A construction barge is tied up at the site of the H.W. Johns-Manville Company in Waukegan in 1919. Johns-Manville purchased 255 acres of unincorporated swampland along Waukegan's lakefront and filled in the land to build its plant, at one time the second-largest of Johns-Manville's 106 plants across the country. Johns-Manville (now Manville Corporation) produces roofing material, rock wool insulation, and corrugated siding, as well as other materials. Courtesy, Waukegan Historical Society

Right: For 40 years, W.C. Petty guided and guarded the education of Lake County's children, as the county's superintendent of schools. He helped modernize a school system that, when he was elected had 65 one-room schools, and when he retired, had but one left. Courtesy, Waukegan News-Sun

donated by Richard Schwartz. Today that school cares for some 90 children daily. Until her death in 1978 Thomas continued to take a personal interest in the children: holding a hand, wiping a tear, or tucking a little one in for a nap.

One of the most powerful and influential figures in politics in those years was a man whose only elected office was that of mayor of Libertyville from 1900 to 1905. Frank Just, who grew up in Waukegan, founded the *Lake County Independent* newspaper (later called the *Independent Register*) in Libertyville in 1892. In 1906 he purchased the *Waukegan Daily Sun,* eventually sold it, and in 1922 started the *Waukegan Daily News.* After an eight-year circulation battle with his former paper, he reacquired the *Sun,* and *The Waukegan News-Sun,* Lake County's only daily newspaper, was born on March 31, 1930. Although a couple of other papers started up during the years, they were short-lived, while *The News-Sun* endures to this day and was owned by the Just family until 1983. Frank Just continued to manage *The News-Sun,* the *Independent Register,* and radio station WKRS until the day he died, May 10, 1953, at the age of 82.

He was eulogized as the "dean of Illinois publishers and a power in the Republican Party." Indeed, a man who was a cub reporter in the late 1940s remembers a conversation between several top, elected county officials in

VOTE FOR

W. C. PETTY

Republican Candidate For

COUNTY SUPERINTENDENT OF SCHOOLS

PRIMARIES, APRIL 8, 1930

perintendent of schools from 1931 to 1971. When he came into office there were 65 one-room schools and when he retired there was only one, Hickory, east of Antioch on Route 173. High schools had increased from eight (Antioch, Barrington, Deerfield-Shields, Ela, Libertyville, Warren, Wauconda, and Waukegan) to 14.

In 1941 Petty was appointed by Gover-

nor Dwight Green to the Illinois Public School Commission to codify all laws pertaining to public schools. In 1960 he organized the Special Education Joint Agreement District of Lake County for the benefit of handicapped children.

This former country school teacher, product of a one-room school himself, was one of five local politicians singled out for praise by State Senator Robert Coulson, a former mayor of Waukegan. Speaking after Watergate, Coulson said Lake County had been served honorably by Petty, and such men as Minard Hulse, circuit court judge, who presided in juvenile court; Gar Leaf, county clerk; August Cepon, Waukegan Township supervisor; and Bernard Decker, a judge of the U.S. District Court and the first Lake County resident to be appointed to the federal bench in 92 years. Decker, a Republican, was appointed by President John F. Kennedy, a Democrat.

On a more entertaining note, Waukegan became a household word nationwide during the 1930s when Jack Benny achieved stardom and mentioned his hometown frequently in his radio skits.

Son of immigrant Lithuanian Jews, Benny Kubelsky was born in a hospital in Chicago on February 14, 1894, and grew up in an apartment above his father's haberdashery on Genesee Street in Waukegan. Although his mother dreamed of his becoming a violin virtuoso, he preferred fiddling away his time at

the Barrison—Waukegan's top vaudeville house—with other local musicians such as future mayor of Waukegan, Frank Wallin. Never much of a student, he went on the road at an early age and adopted the stage name Ben K. Benny. Eventually, after a stint in the Navy where he started doing comedy skits, he became Jack Benny.

In 1934, the year he signed with Jell-O, a poll showed him to be the nation's favorite radio comedian. In 1939 the movie *Man about Town*, starring Benny, premiered at the Genesee Theater in Waukegan. It was a week of celebrating, with the entire cast—which included Dorothy Lamour, Betty Grable, and Phil Harris—in Waukegan for the parade and opening ceremonies.

Benny continued to visit Waukegan through the years, and 25,000 people lined the

Above: *Sprawling grounds on what was then the south end of Libertyville became the site of the 25-bed Elizabeth Condell Memorial Hospital, which opened in 1928. Elizabeth Condell bequeathed most of her estate for the hospital when she died at age 73 in 1917, but stipulated the village would have to raise a $5,000 contribution. A much-expanded Condell Hospital thrives today in central Lake County. Courtesy, Libertyville-Mundelein Historical Society*

Left: *When it opened in 1928, Condell Memorial Hospital in Libertyville showed off its modern, well-equipped operating room. Courtesy, Libertyville-Mundelein Historical Society*

Above: *Newspaper circulation wars were vicious in the early twentieth century, and the* Waukegan Daily Sun *chose to advertise its readership with a large sign atop its two-story brick storefront on North Genesee Street. The* Sun *was purchased by Frank Just in 1906, and was eventually sold by him while he started the* Waukegan Daily News. *Just reacquired it in 1930 to become part of the* Waukegan News-Sun, *a daily newspaper owned by the Just family until 1983. Courtesy, E.W. Plonien Collection, Waukegan Historical Society*

streets to watch him ride in the centennial parade with city officials on June 24, 1959. Before the parade got underway at Belvidere and Genesee streets, Benny asked to see the apartment where he had lived as a boy. According to a biography by his wife, Mary Livingstone Benny, and Hiliard Marks, he found a family living there in adverse conditions. It was much later before anyone in Waukegan learned that upon returning to Hollywood, Benny had arranged to have an entire houseful of new furniture delivered to them.

During that visit, he participated in the groundbreaking for a new junior high school to be named for him. Later, this man who had met presidents and kings, told *The News-Sun,* "My day there . . . was the most thrilling that I have ever experienced throughout my entire career in show business . . ."

Mary Livingstone Benny said, "[Jack] remained all of his life a one-of-a-kind comic actor—a seducer, if you will, of a generation of people who grew up with him through vaudeville, radio, films and television—recipients and participants in a mutual love affair."

While Benny was matching wits with Rochester, his chauffeur in the weekly skits, and promoting strawberry, raspberry, cherry, orange, lemon, and lime (Jell-O) every Sunday night, another young Waukeganite was exploring Waukegan's mysterious and verdant ravines, haunting the public library, and pounding out stories on a miniature toy dial-typewriter in his parents' home on St. James Street. Ray Bradbury lived in Waukegan from his birth in 1920 until he was 14, when he moved to California with his family. He went on to become one of the finest science-fiction writers in the genre's history, according to critics. Like Benny, he also never forgot Waukegan, and in 1957 immortalized it as "Green Town" in the book *Dandelion Wine.* Mary Ann Dadisman, writing in *The News-Sun* said, "*Dandelion Wine* is Bradbury's poem to Waukegan and his boyhood . . . and he has caught it [boyhood here] like a fly in amber."

Bradbury's many titles include *The Martian Chronicles; Fahrenheit 451;* the screenplay for *Moby Dick;* and *Something Wicked This Way Comes,* also based on a childhood experience in Waukegan.

After quietly slipping in and out of town many times through the years, the author was invited back for a public celebration in October 1984. The festivities included productions of his one-act plays by the Waukegan Community Players, a visit with schoolchildren, a tour through the ravine, and a reception.

Dadisman said, "Ray Bradbury left Waukegan 50 years ago but the truth is, in a certain way Waukegan never left him."

Bradbury had said himself in an earlier interview, "What haunts me personally is the smell of the air on a summer night in Waukegan, the lights and noises of a traveling country carnival . . . the brightness of the stars in a Midwestern night."

After the giddiness of the 1920s and the grimness of the 1930s, the inexorable march of events in the rest of the world once more brought the United States into a devastating war.

On December 7, 1941, when Japan attacked Pearl Harbor, there were 8,518 troops stationed at the Great Lakes Naval Training Station. Less than a year later, training capacity had reached 100,000 and by the war's end more than 900,000 recruits had passed through Great Lakes. The station, which had been closed from 1933 to 1935, was expanded by some 1,000 acres and more than 600 buildings.

Thousands of soldiers likewise passed through Fort Sheridan, which served as an induction and separation center. It also was used as an anti-aircraft training facility.

Supposedly, a foreign dignitary said to an American diplomat in 1939, "I see that you folks in the United States are contemplating

Above: *With the pier in the background, the 1938 Waukegan Beach Patrol lifeguards stood ready to assist. Courtesy, Waukegan Historical Society*

Facing page, bottom: *Frank Hampton Just, dean of Lake County publishers and frequently referred to as "the boss" by officials and businessmen alike, began his long newspaper career at age 16 on the Waukegan Weekly Gazette. He is shown with wife Mary and child. Courtesy, Waukegan Historical Society*

Right: *Anna Perry Thomas presides at the first "graduation" of her charges in the new facility of the Happy Day Nursery, built in 1975 with funds raised by the community. Thomas founded the nursery in 1934, during the bleak days of the Depression when children were left alone while parents worked whenever and wherever they could. Some 10 years after Thomas' death in 1978, Happy Day Nursery still cares for 90 children a day. Courtesy, Waukegan Historical Society*

Below: *The sleek interior of the newly built Waukegan National Bank on the southwest corner of Genesee and Washington streets is seen in 1924. The bank, opened in the prosperous days of the 1920s, succumbed to the Depression and closed its doors permanently, along with the Waukegan State Bank. The First National Bank of Waukegan managed to withstand a reportedly heavy run on its resources and still operates today. Courtesy, Waukegan Historical Society*

industrial mobilization. Who's going to run it? God almighty?"

American private industry soon proved itself, rising to near-impossible heights of achievement. In Lake County, every factory geared up for the war effort. The Zion lace factory began turning out mosquito nets. Fansteel's output of tungsten, which was measured in grams in 1940, grew to tons by 1944. American Steel and Wire, which employed 3,000 at its peak, developed a spring to handle the recoil action of 75-millimeter cannons in American airplanes, enabling them to match Germany in the air.

Women in unprecedented numbers went into the factories and the fields to replace men who had gone to war. Although the labor shortage was considered critical in Illinois, no other state in the nation topped its farm or industrial output, according to *Illinois In the Second World War* by Mary Watters. In 1940 there were 854,276 women in the labor force in Illinois and by 1944 there were more than one million.

Americans collected paper, rubber, scrap metal, and, according to Watters, even milkweed pods for life jackets after the supply of kapok was cut off by the war in the Pacific. In Waukegan, Boy Scouts gathered 2,480 pounds of milkweed.

Bonds were once again sold to finance the war effort and in overall quotas, Lake County oversubscribed by 224 percent. At one rally in Libertyville, movie actor James

Cagney served as auctioneer and raised $20,500 for a Hampshire pig.

Lake County was chosen for one of the first blackout tests because it had so quickly and efficiently organized councils under the Office of Civilian Defense. The test, held on January 16, 1942, was declared successful, with Shields Township winning national recognition for its rescue squad. One air raid warden said, ". . . the war no longer seems far off . . ."

More than 13,000 men and 200 women from Lake County served in the armed forces, and 258 lost their lives before *The News-Sun* announced on August 14, 1945: "Japan Surrenders."

"Waukegan roared a thundering, raucous welcome to peace last night," the paper reported the next day, "and the scene was duplicated throughout the county." It was a peaceful celebration, with no property damage reported, and many people simply attended church services or gathered in Waukegan's Powell Park for a municipal band concert.

Above: *When Waukegan chose to name its newest junior high school after Jack Benny, the comedian was deeply moved. He participated in the groundbreaking and returned often to visit the school. Courtesy, Waukegan Sun*

Left: *Jack Benny warms up prior to his appearance as guest violinist with the Waukegan Symphony Orchestra in April 1974. Courtesy, Waukegan Sun*

Right: *Local businesses and industries have always actively supported athletics, and the Washburn-Moen Wire Mill in South Waukegan fielded an indoor baseball team as long ago as 1894-1895. Courtesy, Waukegan Historical Society*

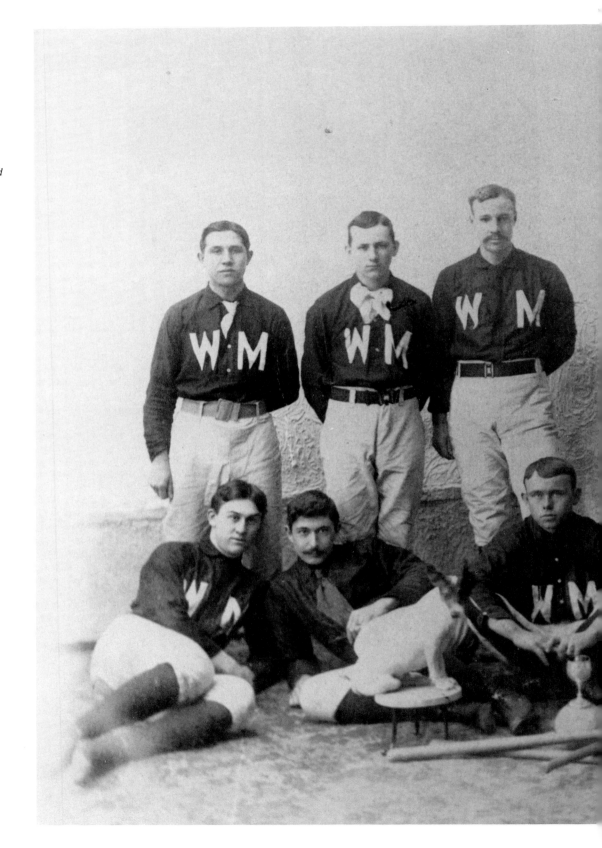

CHAPTER 5

CHARTING
A COURSE

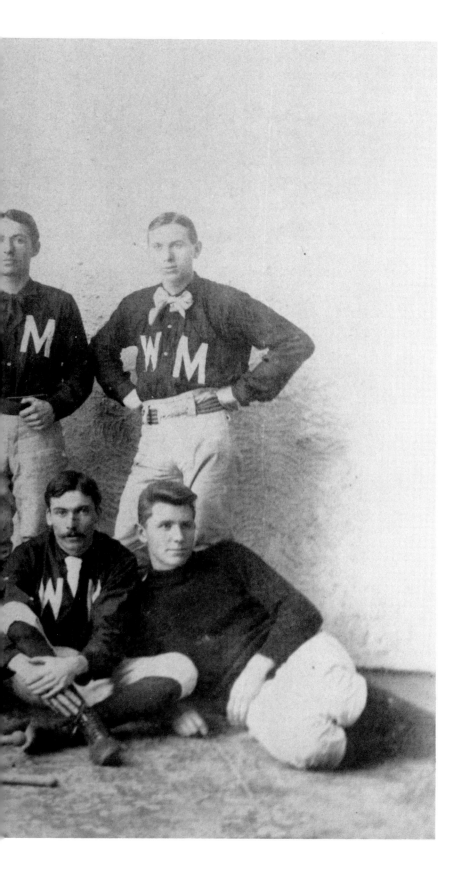

Servicemen returning to Lake County after World War II often found they had no place to call home. The housing shortage was critical, prompting the Lake County Board to create the Lake County Housing Authority in January 1946. The favorable vote followed a presentation by Temple McFayden, a Libertyville contractor and chairman of the state housing authority. The Lake County Housing Authority's first act was to lease Camp Green Bay from the Navy, thus creating more than 2,500 small living units for veterans and their families.

Yet by 1952 the problem was so acute that the federal government moved to energize a 1,500-unit housing project for Lake County, which they designated a "critical defense area." Factories in Waukegan and North Chicago, as well as the Hough Company in Libertyville, needed workers to expand, and those workers needed to be housed, federal authorities said. Therefore, bids were let immediately to private contractors for 1,200 rental and 300 salable units.

Census figures for 1950 showed less than 60 vacant dwellings in Waukegan, either for sale or rent. Nineteen percent of all dwelling units did not have hot water or private baths. In a letter to the editor of *The Waukegan News-Sun,* a woman testified that she had lived in Waukegan for four years, and that the only rental choices she had were two rooms with a shared bath, or a house near Gurnee with an outhouse.

The Waukegan Housing Authority, which had been created in 1949, had by 1951 been dormant for almost a year according to newspaper reports. In response to a federal appeal, it was reactivated by Mayor Robert Coulson, but in October 1954 *The Waukegan News-Sun* reported that after 10 months of wrangling, bickering, and delaying tactics, it was "strangled." The first project built under

Right: *Park City claims its own unique place among Lake County municipalities. Incorporated in 1958, the village encompasses four trailer parks and its population of 3,700 resides in mobile homes and in 250 houses that have since been added within the village. Courtesy, Waukegan News-Sun*

the Waukegan Housing Authority was Barwell Manor in 1966, while the Lake County Housing Authority built its first housing, the Marion Jones Project, in 1964.

People responded to the shortages following the war in various ways. A local historian cited Department of Conservation figures, which showed that the greatest damage to Victorian homes was done immediately after the war when they were carved into smaller units and remodeled rather than renovated.

Within the cities new neighborhoods sprang up: Copeland Manor in Libertyville, Lake County Gardens in Waukegan, and Deerfield Gardens in Deerfield. Around the lakes to the west of Lake County, young couples turned summer cottages into year-round homes. Whole new subdivisions sprouted, such as Wildwood on the Gages Lake site of the former Sears' (scion of the retailing giant) estate, where Gunnison homes were erected. Those pre-fabs—developed in the 1930s—were first erected in sizable numbers in this area, according to a resident.

Townships burgeoned. Avon experienced 300 percent growth between 1940 and 1950, and Benton, Fremont, Grant, Lake Villa, and Wauconda all doubled.

Towns grew out of cornfields, and one look at the number of incorporations in the 1950s ascertains this: Island Lake, 1951; Lindenhurst and Long Grove, 1956; Lincolnshire and Deer Park, 1957; Park City, Hawthorn Woods, Kildeer, Vernon Hills, Indian Creek, and Old Mill Creek, 1958; and Third Lake, North Barrington, Lake Barrington, and Barrington Hills, 1959. To be sure, many were so-called "paper communities," which relied on the county or neighboring towns to supply services. These communities predated the 1969 law requiring a 2,500 minimum population in order to be incorporated, subject to veto by surrounding communities, or a 7,500 minimum to be immune to veto. They were created because people wanted to control their own destinies rather than be governed by the county or annexed by a neighboring city.

Unique among the new municipalities was Park City. It was composed almost entirely of four trailer parks, in 2 ½ square miles of Waukegan and Warren townships. Despite much opposition from the city of Waukegan and neighboring school districts, 389 of the 400 eligible voters went to the polls, and incorporation won by 331 votes. One immediate effect was that state license fees for trailer parks were no longer applicable.

In the 30 years since its incorporation, Park City has grown from 1,250 to 3,700. Although four trailer parks remain, today there are also some 250 houses, as opposed to about 5 in 1958.

As the towns grew, the farms shrank. The North Barrington and Lake Barrington incorporations alone, with their estate-like homes, removed some 2,200 acres of farmland. In 1900 there were more than 259,000 acres of land under cultivation in Lake County. By 1950 that figure had shrunk to slightly more than 173,000, while the population had escalated from 34,504 in 1900 to 179,097 in 1950. By 1960 it had reached 293,656.

Whole populations began to move. According to a sociological study by the American Jewish Committee, the numbers of Jews in Highland Park grew from an insignificant minority before World War II to one out of every three households afterward. Most, the report said, were prosperous and highly educated. The original Jewish community had included the very wealthy, attracted to Highland Park at the turn of the century by open housing and a luxurious golf club with open membership. Among them was Julius Rosenwald, the catalog-merchandising genius of Sears Roebuck.

Waukegan's population in 1940 was 34,241. In 1950, probably due to the housing crunch, it had risen by only 4,000, but by 1960 it had soared to 55,719. In 1950 slightly more than 50 percent of the blacks in Lake County lived in Waukegan, North Chicago, and Zion. By 1960 those communities were home to more than 80 percent of the black population.

Hispanics were not even counted separately in the 1950 census, although there are records dating back to the 1800s of families of Mexican origin in Waukegan. During the Second World War many Puerto Ricans came to the area to work in the factories, or as domestics on the North Shore. The more recent breakdown of the economy in Mexico has led to an influx of immigrants from south of the border.

Official census figures for those claiming Spanish as their mother tongue showed 1,122 in Lake County in 1960. In 10 years the number increased eightfold and by 1980, when they were first categorized according to the country of their origin, the census counted 3,680 Puerto Ricans, 13,657 Mexicans, and 3,727 others in Lake County. Social agencies and those who minister to Hispanics claim there are many thousands more than the official figures show. They are concentrated mainly in the industrialized areas of Waukegan, North Chicago, and Zion, and in Highwood, Round Lake, and the Diamond Lake area of Mundelein.

According to *But Not Next Door* by Harry and David Rosen, housing in Deerfield—population 15,000 with no blacks—came into the national spotlight in 1959 when developer Morris Milgram, with government approval, proposed an integrated subdivision based on ratios. Contractors were engaged and model homes put up even as the uproar by citizens of the commuter-community reached fever pitch. Neighbor turned against neighbor when those in favor of the project formed a human rights group. Finally the powers that be

Below: *Commonwealth Edison built its $250-million nuclear powered generating plant on the shores of Lake Michigan in Zion, within a mile of the city's residential area and just north of the Illinois Beach State Park. Dedicated in 1973, the facility has drawn its share of protesters and admirers in its 15-year history. Courtesy, Waukegan News-Sun*

Sunbathers on the shores of Illinois Beach State Park at Lake Michigan catch their "rays" in the shadow of Commonwealth Edison's nuclear powered generating station in Zion. Courtesy, Waukegan News-Sun

had a solution. Ninety-five percent of the voters went to the polls on December 21, 1959, to vote on whether to allow the Deerfield Park District to issue bonds for the purpose of purchasing or condemning additional land for parks. The land the district wanted, of course, included the new developments.

The results were 2,635 in favor to 1,230 against. The subdivisions, one of which was ironically named Floral Park, were promptly condemned and the case moved into the courts, not ending until the United States Supreme Court ruled against the builders in June 1963. In the meantime Eleanor Roosevelt, who had been in Chicago for a meeting, came out to Deerfield to congratulate those who had stood up for integration. By 1980 the population of Deerfield had grown only to 17,000—44 of

whom were black. However, in all fairness to Deerfield, it was not the only community in Lake County which overtly discouraged open housing during that era.

As the population concentrated in urban areas, the need for places where one could "breathe free" became apparent. On November 24, 1958, the Lake County Forest Preserve District was created by general referendum. After several years of organizing and raising money bolstered by federal funds, the first land purchase—Van Patten Woods on the Des Plaines River in the northwestern part of the county—was made. This was followed by the purchase of Daniel Wright Woods, south of Libertyville. Dr. Rolland Sandee, a member of the Lake County Board and Forest Preserve District Board from 1959 to 1981, said that

Left: *Lake County has fielded a few professional baseball players in its time. One of its early starts was Ernie Krueger of Waukegan, shown catching behind Babe Ruth in a 1921 game. Krueger started his career as a bat boy for the Chicago Cubs, played in a World Series with the Cleveland Indians, played with the New York Giants, and as a Brooklyn Dodger in 1920 caught in the longest game in history, a 26-inning marathon against the Boston Braves. Courtesy, Waukegan Historical Society*

10 sites—mainly along the Des Plaines River—were targeted in those early years and that by 1978 all had been acquired. They include Lake County's forests, prairies, wetlands, dunes, ravines, floodplains, lakes, and streams, and encompass 12,000 acres.

Included in these acres are the Ryerson Conservation Area, once the home and estate of steel baron Edward L. Ryerson, in the area first settled by Daniel Wright; Lakewood Forest Preserve, where the Lake County Museum is located; a recreational trail under construction along the length of the Des Plaines; and the acquisition of open space along the two branches of the Skokie River, which according to Sandee will eventually be used for retention basins to prevent flooding.

Dunelands north of Waukegan were deemed valuable for their unique flora, wildlife, and beauty as early as 1888 by Waukegan nurseryman Robert Douglas and landscape architect Jens Jensen, who considered them for a park. In 1914 Dean Howard Ganster, rector of Christ Episcopal Church in Waukegan, urged the city to purchase the land, to no avail. An early association leased some of the land and opened it to picnickers and naturalists on a daily-fee basis.

The government also had an interest in the area. As early as the Civil War, Camp Logan in the dunes was used as a prisoner of war camp. It also was used as a training site during both world wars. In 1950 concerned naturalists formed the Dunesland Preservation Society and in 1961, according to *The Waukegan News-Sun,* were successful in challenging Waukegan's bid to buy the property for a golf course.

Soon after, the first 900 acres were acquired by the state and designated a nature preserve. It was recognized by the U.S. Park Service and the Department of Interior as a national landmark. Acquisition of Camp Logan and privately owned land followed, and the park now encompasses 4,160 acres stretching along 6 ½ miles of Lake Michigan. It is abutted on the north by the Lake County Forest Preserve District's Spring Bluff site.

For several years Illinois Beach State Park has been the top draw among state parks. In 1987 more than 2 million people used it, one million more visitors than the runner-up received.

Private ownership of a large block of land is credited to steel industrialist Tempel Smith, who started buying farms in the Old Mill Creek area in the late 1950s. He also imported for breeding the famed Lipizzan horses. By the time he died in 1980 he was said to have owned 7,000 acres: most of the village of Old Mill Creek, which has no municipal center and is, in essence, a community of farms. Smith's Lipizzans, famed for their dressage or ballet-like movements, performed for charitable events and in the inaugural parades of Richard Nixon and Ronald Reagan. Since Smith's

death, the family has opened Tempel Farms to the public during the summer for regularly scheduled performances by the graceful animals.

Federal subsidies for road building programs—which flourished during the Eisenhower administration—were in part responsible for the growth of Lake County commuter communities in the decades following World War II. A new concept was also introduced to the state when the Illinois State Toll Highway Commission (now the Illinois State Toll Authority) was established by an act of the legislature in 1953 and empowered to issue revenue bonds and build 187 miles of road. The result included the Tri-State Tollway, which goes south from Wisconsin through Lake County and loops around the bottom of

Lake Michigan to Indiana. With land acquired and money raised, construction began in January 1957 and was completed 19 months later.

Some commuters preferred to leave their cars at home and take public transportation. John Conolly of Gurnee and Waukegan, who had been elected to the Illinois House of Representatives in 1962 at the age of 27, was eulogized in 1987 as the "chief architect of the Regional Transportation Authority (RTA)." This governmental body, which encompasses six northeastern Illinois counties, was established by referendum on March 19, 1974, to coordinate the services of the Chicago Transit Authority, commuter railroads, and the suburban bus companies. Conolly's unwavering belief in the RTA, which was a highly controversial issue, is believed to have cost him his seat in the legislature. Interestingly, Conolly's great-great-grandfather, David Ballentine, was one of the men who were instrumental in first bringing rail service to Waukegan.

Throughout its history, the RTA has been well-served by board members from Lake County. As part of a recent reorganization, which recognized the RTA as the umbrella organization to oversee the budgets of the three divisions while leaving operational procedure up to them, Samuel K. Skinner of Lake Forest was appointed chairman.

The eyes of America have been turned skyward since the Wright brothers took off from Kitty Hawk in 1903. Charles Lindberg became a national hero when he flew across the Atlantic in 1927. But it was not until World War II that aviation came out of the age of barnstorming and into its own. Thomas Booth of Waukegan was one barnstormer who recognized its potential, and in 1943 he started the Lake County Airport on farmland north of Waukegan. After the establishment of the Waukegan Port District by the state legislature in 1955 (the first in the state authorized to construct and operate an airport) Booth was bought out, and the name was changed to the Waukegan Memorial Airport. F. Ward Just was appointed the first chairman of the district. In 1959 the district achieved the distinction of refunding some $600 to the state, from a $75,000 appropriation they had received two years earlier.

Today the airport, renamed the Waukegan Regional Airport in 1985, boasts a 6,000-foot runway capable of handling large corporate jets, 13 corporate hangars, an instrument landing system, and a traffic-control tower. According to a 1988 newspaper report, corporate jets fly well over 2,000 business operations out of Waukegan each year, some of them nonstop to Europe.

Catapulted into the atomic age by the war, Lake County became one of the sites for a nuclear-powered generating plant in the 1960s. Commonwealth Edison, one of the first private-industry groups to study the generating of electricity from the atom with the approval of the Atomic Energy Commission, in 1967 announced plans for a $250-million facility in Zion, the largest in the world at that

time. From the beginning, it had its supporters and detractors. At the dedication on October 5, 1973, Zion mayor Bruce Dunbar exulted in the increase of sales tax revenue: $300,000 in 1972 as opposed to $180,000 in 1967, according to Art Peterson, *News-Sun* reporter.

Things soured somewhat over the years, and in 1984 *The News-Sun* reported that Zion-area taxing bodies had been ordered to pay back $5.1 million to Commonwealth Edison as the result of an out-of-court settlement on the value and tax assessment of the power plant from 1975 to 1983.

Concerns over the safety of the plant escalated following the Three Mile Island accident in Pennsylvania in 1979, causing the regulatory commission to appoint an on-site inspector. However, many people remain uneasy about long-term effects as well as day-to-day safety.

Nor has the cost of electricity in this area been reduced, as promised when the plant was first proposed. It is, in fact, far higher than in the neighboring state of Wisconsin.

The number of people pursuing college degrees escalated following the war, due to unprecedented prosperity and the availability of federal grants for veterans. The idea for a junior college first surfaced in 1962, according to Ruth Rickard in *History of the College of Lake County 1969-1986*. At the first referendum in 1964, a Lake County district was turned down by a slim margin. Redrawing district lines to exclude Highland Park, Lake Forest, Barrington, Deerfield, and Adlai Stevenson high school districts, the community college association called for a second referendum in 1967. The district was approved by a two-to-one ratio. It had been guided to that point, Rickard said, by people like Roy Jones, president of the North Shore Gas Company; Dr. Jack Adams, superintendent of Millburn Grade School; and James Lonergan, Abbott Laboratories executive.

Temporary offices for the new College of Lake County (CLC) were in the St. Therese Hospital School of Nursing, with an early understanding between the hospital and the board that the college would eventually take over the hospital's nurse training program. In May 1968, land developers A. Harold Anderson and Paul W. Brandel donated 181

Facing page: The expanded facilities of the Waukegan Regional Airport have been welcomed in particular by nearby corporations, who now fly more than 2,000 business trips annually in company-owned jets, some to distant destinations in Europe. The airport began operating in 1955 under the auspices of the Waukegan Port District. It features a 6,000-foot runway, traffic control tower and instrument landing system. Photo by Mary Carmody

acres on the Avon-Warren Township line. The site, easily accessible by roads, was three miles east of the geographical center of the district and one mile west of the projected 1985 population center. It has since been annexed to Grayslake, which has managed to remain an authentically quiet, rural town since its incorporation in 1895.

Temporary buildings were hastily thrown up and, in a field of mud on a wind-swept prairie, classes opened on September 25, 1969. With 2,360 students, it was the largest opening of any Illinois junior college to that date. In just one year, enrollment almost doubled. Today, in permanent buildings completed in 1974 and two outreach centers, more than 12,000 students are enrolled in the Grayslake-based school.

State law now mandates that every high school district must belong to a community college district by 1990. The high school districts excluded from the 1967 referendum, according to Rickard, had hoped to align themselves into a separate district. As those hopes failed to materialize they joined the CLC district one by one, with the exception of Lake Forest. However, the Lake Forest High School District is obliged to pay the difference between in-district and out-of-the-district tuition for any of its students who choose to attend CLC.

Trinity College, which can trace its history to 1897 when members of the Swedish Evangelical Free Church of Chicago founded a Bible school in their church basement, expanded its four-year program in 1956 to include liberal arts majors. The formerly affiliated seminary was granted a separate charter as Trinity Divinity School. Both relocated to a modern 105-acre campus in Bannockburn in 1965.

Despite the number of colleges in Lake County and its high-income profile, the only graduate-degree programs available are in business, from the Lake Forest Graduate School of Management; theology, from the University of St. Mary of the Lake; and medicine and health sciences from the University of Health Sciences/The Chicago Medical School, which moved from Chicago to North Chicago in 1980.

Finally out from under the clouds of de-

pression and war, people were ready to laugh and play and be entertained. They took to the water in increasing numbers, and in 1962 Fox Lake was the setting for a Governor's Cup Regatta. The first drive-in theater in the county opened in Waukegan in 1949. The Music Center of Lake County (now Jack Benny Center for the Arts) was started in 1964.

From August 27 to September 7, 1959, Lake County was host to the Pan American Games. The rifle event took place on the Waukegan lakefront, the pistol shoot at Great Lakes, and the equestrian and cross-country contests at Libertyville.

Over the years sports have figured prominently in the fabric of life in Lake County: sand-lot baseball teams, high school basketball competition, and industrial bowling leagues. Some local stars made it into the big time. Among them are: Bob O'Farrell of Waukegan, who threw out Babe Ruth while playing for the St. Louis Cardinals in the World Series of 1926 and was declared that year's most valuable National League player; Otto Graham from Waukegan Township High School, who, as quarterback, led the Cleveland Browns to four world championships and won himself a slot in the Football Hall of Fame; Jim McMillen, who played for the Chicago Bears, wrestled professionally in such places as Madison Square Garden in New York, and came home to serve as mayor of Antioch from 1950 to 1956; Billy McKinney, vice president of basketball operations for the Chicago Bulls, who starred on the courts of Zion-Benton High School before going on to Northwestern University and then a career with the pros; and Andrea Yaeger of Lincolnshire, a tennis pro who at the age of 18 became the highest-paid athlete in Chicago and ended 1983 as a semi-finalist at Wimbledon, where she handed Billie Jean King her worst defeat ever.

It was like the big time in Waukegan after World War II, when the Waukegan Merchants semi-pro football team organized and joined the Central States League. Made up of men from all over the county, they played home games at Weiss Field and were title contenders until their disbandment in the mid-1950s.

A decade later the Lake County Rifles, a minor league professional football team, was formed with 40 local owners. When the team was picked up by Meister Brau Breweries, talent was recruited from all over the country. After Meister Brau went into receivership the team struggled along for two years, playing their last game in 1973 as league champions.

On the political scene in those halcyon years there was well-to-do Chicago lawyer Adlai Stevenson, who hobnobbed with the wealthy of Lake Forest and became known internationally for his statesmanship, wit, and oratorical ability. Grandson of an earlier Adlai (who had been Grover Cleveland's vice president), he grew up in downstate Bloomington and started to move into politics in the FDR years. From the time he and his wife built their first home in rural Libertyville in 1936, he considered Lake County his home. Even though much of his last years was spent on the road, engaged in his country's business, he loved to return to the farm. (The property, which later became a part of incorporated Mettawa, now belongs to the Forest Preserve District.)

Stevenson served as governor from 1949 to 1953 and, according to Robert P. Howard, acquired a reputation for improving the moral climate in Illinois. Yet he was defeated by Dwight Eisenhower twice in bids for the presi-

dency. In the 1952 election, 94 percent of Lake County's 93,000 registered voters went to the polls and cast 54,800 ballots for Eisenhower. Consequently Stevenson was appointed ambassador to the United Nations in 1961, serving until his death in 1965. A newspaper headline at the time proclaimed: "First Gentleman of the World Dies."

While Stevenson was governor, Robert

Above: *Governor Adlai Ewing Stevenson II of Libertyville casts his vote for president in his home precinct in 1952, the year Gen. Dwight D. Eisenhower first defeated Stevenson for president of the United States. Courtesy,* Waukegan News-Sun

Left: *It was "the farm" in rural Libertyville Township which Adlai Stevenson called home. Purchased in 1937 because it was near enough to his Chicago law office, Stevenson's home became his haven from the pressures of life as a world statesman. Here he walked along the banks of the adjacent Des Plaines River with his dogs, or tended his sheep and horses. "It is very much home because I built it out of field and forest," Stevenson was quoted as saying. The house and property are now owned by the Lake County Forest Preserve, and have since been incorporated into the village of Mettawa. Courtesy,* Waukegan News-Sun

Right: *From the time she was appointed the first woman to serve on the state attorney's staff in 1958, State Senator Adeline Geo-Karis has continued to make history. She served in the Illinois House of Representatives from 1973 to 1980, was then elected state senator, and now also holds the office of Mayor of the City of Zion. Parade-goers are fond of remembering the Greece-born Sen. Geo-Karis walking the route while other politicians rode in open-air convertibles for a while. Now they, too, walk. Courtesy* Waukegan News-Sun

Coulson was doing his own bit to improve morals in Waukegan. Elected mayor in 1949, he became known as a foe of gambling, using a then revolutionary method of revoking a liquor license to enforce gambling laws. He also was said, by *The Waukegan News-Sun,* to be the first mayor in the U.S. to combine water and sewer systems in order to use the bonding power and collection machinery of one to finance the maintenance of the other.

Following two terms in Waukegan Coulson served in the Illinois House and Senate, where he was successively whip and majority leader. After he failed to get a bill passed, to license distribution of ammunition as a crime deterrent, a fellow legislator asked, "What next?"

"Oh, I've got a few wild ideas left," Coulson is said to have replied. Not so wild were his early voice-in-the-wilderness proposals: to give Vietnam veterans a bonus, to clean up our waterways, and to include black history in U.S. history courses. A graduate of Dartmouth University and of the University of Chicago who had been born in Grayslake in 1912, Coulson finished his distinguished career writing college texts on government and literature. He died in 1986.

Gambling, as had illegal booze before it, continued to plague the county, and in 1957 a young state's attorney figured prominently in a number of raids against the slot machines. He was Thomas Moran, and was destined to rise through the judicial ranks to be elected chief justice of the Supreme Court of Illinois in 1987. Moran is the grandson of Tom Tyrell, who as Waukegan police chief personified the law for several generations of citizens.

On the state's attorney's staff in 1958 was an assistant who made history by being the first woman appointed to that position in the county—Adeline Geo-Karis. Born in Greece and educated in Chicago, where she earned a law degree from DePaul University, Geo-Karis also was the first woman elected to the office of justice of the peace in Waukegan. It was only the first triumph in a career of political successes. Geo-Karis served in the Illinois House of Representatives from 1973 to 1980. She has been in the senate since 1981, where she was the first woman appointed to a leadership position. In addition, she has held

the office of mayor of Zion since 1988. Among legislation she sponsored were bills on nuclear safety, a repeal of the Illinois inheritance tax law, and the allowance of guilty-but-mentally-ill verdicts.

John Matijevich also achieved success in politics against great odds. He has repeatedly been elected to the Illinois House as a Democrat, in a county that gives short shrift to most Democrats. His election initially was made possible by the unique cumulative-voting procedure then in effect in Illinois. Under this method, voters with three slots to fill could vote for only one candidate, and have that vote count as three.

A son of Croatian immigrants, Matijevich was born and reared in North Chicago, where he served as police chief and magistrate successively before going to Springfield in 1966. Never having lost an election since, he is currently house assistant majority leader. Unsuccessfully, he twice sponsored the Equal Rights Amendment in the house. Called a "concerned and caring guy" by a political reporter, he also has been instrumental in the passage of mental health bills and the regulation of summer camps.

Although W.J. Murphy tended to downplay the importance of the West Lake County Bloc in politics, there is no doubt in most people's minds that it existed or that he was one of its most powerful figures. Hailing from Antioch Township, with business interests in Round Lake, he vied unsuccessfully in 1950 for the Congressional seat of Ralph Church— only to be beaten by Church's widow,

Marguerite Stitt Church, the first woman to represent Lake County and northern Cook County in Congress.

Murphy was elected to the Illinois Legislature in 1954, and served for 18 years. During his tenure he was house majority leader and whip. After being defeated in a half-hearted run in the 1974 primaries, he turned around and defeated the powerful Robert Milton of Lake Forest for GOP party chairmanship.

Murphy himself said, according to an article in *The Waukegan News-Sun* in 1974, "I did become one of the greatest wheeler-dealers and the greatest horsetrader . . . in the whole gosh-darned General Assembly." Despite his many successes in sponsoring worthwhile legislation, he was never able to get a constitutional amendment passed legalizing bingo. But for his persistent efforts, he was dubbed "Bingo Bill" by Chicago newspapers.

Hailing from the same region was William G. Stratton, the first Illinois governor with Lake County roots and the youngest in 70 years when he took office in 1953. The son of a former secretary of state and a Lake County school teacher, Stratton was born in Ingleside in 1914. He attended the one-room Shady Lane School on the site of his grandfather's farm, but moved from the area before entering politics in the 1940s.

Late in the 1950s a political phenomenon burst onto the local scene in the person of Robert Sabonjian. On the morning after the Waukegan mayoral election in 1957, *Waukegan News-Sun* reporter Ralph Zahorik asked, along with everyone else in town, how this man who was now the mayor had won. With no platform or headquarters, Sabonjian preferred to stand on streetcorners and hand out his literature. He ran against the Republicans and denounced the Democrats; he blasted gamblers and insulted minorities; and he spent only $800 on his campaign.

Born in Waukegan in 1916 to immigrant Armenian parents, Sabonjian grew up on the South Side, where his election was regarded as one of the local boys making good uptown. Perhaps this sense of South Side solidarity was what the policymakers failed to take into account when they wrote off Sabonjian early in the campaign. It was the last time they did that, and by 1975 Zahorik was calling the five-term mayor "the most powerful politician in Waukegan and perhaps Lake County."

Nicknamed "The Rock," he has been called blunt and belligerent, but never dull. He kept his finger on the pulse of the people and, according to *The Mayor's Mandate* by Ann L. Greer, spent 70 percent of his day finding jobs for citizens.

All through the hot summer of 1966, American cities were torn by race riots. The violence came to Waukegan on August 27 in the form of 350 rioters who smashed windows, dumped garbage, and exploded firecrackers. Before it was over four days later, many had been injured and a child severely burned by a fire bomb tossed into a car. Sabonjian raced home from a California vacation and immediately clamped a curfew on the South Side. He deemed the rioters a "small minority of undesirables and scum," and promised to take steps to cut off their public aid and evict them from public housing.

Black community leaders asked for an apology and, getting none, two of them consequently resigned from the mayor's commission on human rights. In the meantime, mothers continued picketing at Whittier School, which some thought had sparked the riots in the first place.

Left: *Antioch Township resident W.J. Murphy was one of the most powerful politicians in the West Lake County block. Murphy served for 18 years in the state legislature, including acting as house majority leader and majority whip. His nickname of "Bingo Bill" came from his efforts to legalize bingo in the state of Illinois, something he never quite managed. Courtesy,* Waukegun News-Sun

Circuit Court Associate Judge Charles S. Parker had found the Waukegan School Board in violation of the state Armstrong Act on July 26. The Armstrong Act required school boards to periodically reassess their boundaries, and the Waukegan board was ordered to submit a plan by August 1 to end the racial imbalance at Whittier School. Instead, the board appealed.

The suit against the board had been brought by two white and two black parents—Shirley Tometz, Marvin Smith, the Reverend H.J. Cook, and Violet Rukstales—backed by the Waukegan-area Conference on Religion and Race. The case went all the way to the Illinois Supreme Court, which first ruled for the school board. Then in a first-time ever reversal, on May 29, 1968, the court ruled for the parents.

Sabonjian, on the strength of his "law-and-order stand" during the riots, ran an unsuccessful write-in campaign for U.S. senator in the fall of 1966. He garnered 7,000 votes in Lake County.

Another confrontation in the summer of 1970 saw Sabonjian pitted against his own police officers, who went on strike for the right to be represented by the Cook County Police Association. After a month, 54 bitter police officers were found by the Waukegan Civil Service Commission to be in violation of commission rules and were fired. Sabonjian had won another round.

But in 1977 he was defeated by Bill Morris and blamed it on the times: Watergate, Vietnam, and young people against the establishment. After the election Sabonjian said to Morris, "This is my town as well as your town so I wish you the best of luck."

Later, when asked why he didn't retire to a warm climate, Sabonjian replied, "When you walk down the street in Hawaii they are not going to call you, 'Mayor.'" Perhaps it was that desire to be called "Mayor," to be the boss, that led to Sabonjian's comeback in 1985. At the age of 69, he defeated Morris—9,793 to 8,229.

Rather quietly, without much effect on the domestic scene, Lake County members of the armed forces went to Korea in 1950 and returned in 1953. For those who served and for their families the war, termed a "police ac-

tion," was all too real, but for most citizens it was a faraway battle limited to the headlines. Communism at home seemed more of a threat than communism in Korea.

It was a far different story in the 1960s when the civil rights marches in the South were followed by student and civic demonstrations across the country, protesting U.S. involvement in Vietnam. In Lake County, a college junior home for the summer of 1968 brought the antiwar movement to blue-collar Waukegan when he handed out antidraft handbills at a shopping center. Town forces reacted immediately. The police arrested him, the newspaper denounced him in an editorial, and the mayor ranted about beatniks. However, the young man was defended by members of the clergy and other prominent citizens, one of whom wrote to the editor of the paper, "these young people who are not afraid to be counted give me renewed faith that . . . a true sense of morality is developing among the young generation."

As feelings against the war escalated, 200 Waukegan High School students staged a protest march the following year, and a group that called itself Mothers for Peace demonstrated at a Memorial Day observance.

The veterans of the bitter conflict came back in twos and threes, and there were no welcoming parades. By the time the last U.S. troops left Vietnam in 1973 the country wanted to wipe the war out of its mind, but Lake County could not forget. The wounded were in the Veterans Administration Medical Center in North Chicago, and for the families and friends of those who had died—99, according to a *News-Sun* tabulation—there was no forgetting.

"But most of the people were not interested [in Vietnam] and there was no point in talking about it," veteran Tony Gordon said. Although he and about 30 other veterans banded together at the College of Lake County for camaraderie, they were mainly focused on the future: their educations and careers.

The turnaround in the public attitude toward the war seemingly began at the time the Vietnam Veterans Memorial was dedicated in Washington, D.C., in 1982. In Lake County $10,000 was raised toward the construction of a state memorial in Springfield, which was dedicated on the eve of Mother's Day 1988.

Monument to another age, the picturesque, old courthouse in the square in Waukegan was the scene of some strange goings-on in the 1960s. But none was more bizarre than the election of November 1964, with its infamous orange ballot in addition to four other ballots of varying hues. Because Governor Otto Kerner had vetoed reapportionment, candidates had to run at large for the legislature, a first in the nation's history. Each party had 118 candidates listed on the long, long, paper ballot.

The orange ballot boxes were taken to the National Guard Armory in Waukegan. There, 22 four-person teams worked in staggered shifts around the clock for eight days, counting the ballots by hand.

The time finally came when not one more person or piece of paper could be stuffed into the old courthouse, and an annex was opened across the street. In 1958 the Lake County Board of Supervisors appealed to the voters to approve a $2.5-million bond issue for expansion of the courthouse, but it was rejected. Board members pondered the problem for two years, and in 1960 decided to take advantage of a state law and form the Lake County Public Building Commission. The title to Courthouse Square was transferred to this five-person group, which was authorized to sell bonds to build buildings and then rent them to the county. The commission is still in operation, with its present lease due to run until 2005.

After much squabbling over where to build the new facility, with other townships resurrecting old bids for a more central location, construction of a 10-story administration building began on the original site. Two other stages of construction included a five-story jail, and a three-story courts building.

On October 9, 1967, county board members met for the first time in their new 10th-floor offices—on $285 leather chairs. This caused great consternation among voters, who were shocked by such extravagance. There were 36 chairs, the exact number needed by the supervisors and assistant supervisors. This was considered shortsighted by some, but in light of the 1972 state law which eliminated assistants and designated the office of member

Left: *When the new Lake County Courthouse was being built in the mid-1960s, little did the public know that a costly legal battle would ensue over faulty construction work. The $12 million complex, completed in 1970, was found to have a leaky roof, faulty beams in the jail wing, and buckling in the outdoor plaza. Taxpayers ended up paying more than half of the cost of repairs to the 10-story building. Twenty years later, the county has outgrown the jail facility, and is building a new one in Waukegan. Courtesy, Waukegan News-Sun*

of the county board as separate from that of supervisor, 36 chairs proved to be more than enough.

With the administration tower completed and the jail under way, the 90-year-old courthouse which sat between the two was demolished in 1968. In a last gasp, part of its third floor slid into the new building, but no serious damage was done.

The $12-million complex was completed in 1970, and from the beginning was plagued with problems. The roof over the courts leaked. To the west, the plaza leaked and buckled. Faulty beams in the jail made exterior brick-facing unsafe. And in 1973 a grand jury called to investigate problems in the jail reported, "[The jail] seems to have been constructed with total disregard for the treatment of inmates . . ."

Repairs totaled more than $700,000. After battling back and forth in the courts, the voters were left to pick up almost $400,000 of the tab.

However, no one would argue that the buildings are magnificent, replete with marble and black walnut paneling. And the view from the top is unparalleled. On a clear day one can see to Chicago.

Right: *In 1844, 64,000 bushels of wheat were shipped out of Little Fort Harbor, a harbinger of what was to come for Waukegan, whose name is the Potawatomi equivalent of "trading post." Today's modern harbor, expanded in 1985 to create a South Harbor Marina, is a busy home for commercial and pleasure craft alike. Large cruisers still bring industrial supplies to factories, and commercial fishing is a profitable enterprise in the waters of Lake Michigan. Photo by Mary Carmody*

CHAPTER 6

ON THE CREST OF THE WAVE

In many ways, the year 1970 was a turning point for Lake County. For one thing voters, following a statewide pattern, endorsed the ratification of the first new Illinois constitution in 100 years, 34,920 votes to 26,172.

County delegates to the state constitutional convention included Mary Pappas of Lake Bluff, a lawyer; Jeannette Mullen of Barrington, who was active in the League of Women Voters; and John Wenum of Lake Forest, a professor of government at Lake Forest College. In a clever move to ensure passage of the document, delegates presented four controversial measures to the voters as separate proposals. Three of the proposals—to lower the voting age to 18 for state elections, to abolish the death penalty, and to have judges appointed rather than elected—were turned down. The continuation of minority representation (the election of three representatives from each district regardless of size) was the fourth proposal, and it was passed. The vote in Lake County on all four issues followed the statewide pattern.

The new constitution included a bill of rights for housing and employment, and ordered financial disclosure by political candidates. It abolished personal property taxes, created a single state board of education for kindergarten through graduate school, and required the governor and lieutenant governor to be members of the same party. This posed problems for Adlai Stevenson III when he ran for governor in 1986. A follower of extremist Lyndon LaRouche won the primary bid for lieutenant governor on the Democratic ticket. Stevenson, refusing to run with someone of that political bent, formed a third party and eventually lost the election.

On November 4, 1970, Grace Mary

Right: *Waukegan Mayor Robert Sabonjian, nick-named "The Rock," spent $800 on his first mayoral campaign in 1957, and with no platform, no head-quarters, and little political backing, launched what be-came a five-term stint as the city's chief executive. During his tenure, he fired striking police officers, called race rioters "scum," and took his law-and-order stand to a write-in cam-paign for the U.S. Senate. Defeated in 1977 after 20 years in office, Sabonjian returned in 1985 to oust the man who had defeated him. Photo by Mary Carmody*

Facing page, bottom: *The sprawling headquarters of Abbott Laboratories at Abbott Park near North Chicago include nearly 3,000,000 square feet of floor space, a far cry from the tiny kitchen where Dr. Wallace C. Abbott, a neighborhood physician in Ravenswood, Illinois, be-gan to manufacture a new kind of pill in 1888. As Abbott's celebrated its 100th anniversary in 1988, the pharmaceutical firm had 24 manufacturing, research and distribution facilities in the United States, employed 38,000 people worldwide, had op-erations in 41 countries and 1988 sales of more than $4 million. Photo by Mary Carmody*

Stern, who as assistant supervisor on the county board had been needling old-guard politicians for several years, ran for county clerk under the slogan, "she's not one of the boys," and was elected. She was the first Dem-ocrat elected to a Lake County office in a third of a century, and only the fourth since the Civil War.

The previous Democrat, Russ Alford, had been elected county clerk in November 1934 by defeating incumbent Lew Hendee. However, the canvassing board found Hendee to be the winner by 147 votes. Alford promptly filed suit for a writ of mandamus to command the board to allow him to take office. Judge Ralph Dady ruled for Alford but Hendee ap-pealed, and while the appeal was pending it was not required that Alford be sworn into of-fice along with the other November winners. The case dragged on for a year before it was resolved and Alford installed into office. He was scarcely in office when he was sharply criticized in the newspaper for his handling of an election.

The first suit in Waukegan alleging ra-cial discrimination in the sale of a house was brought in 1970, but a federal court ruled that none had occurred. The Waukegan Human Relations Commission was formed in 1968 but, according to *The News-Sun*, it heard only

four complaints by 1970, and those had been brought in the first two months after its cre-ation. The picture painted by some people of Waukegan, as one of the worst towns in terms of racially segregated areas, seemed to be turning around.

One breakthrough came in 1968—the year the first open housing law of the twentieth century was passed by Congress. The U.S. De-partment of Defense ordered an end to racial discrimination in housing for military person-nel and required landlords renting to them to sign pledges to that effect. Mayor Sabonjian called a meeting of all landlords in the city, some of whom were threatening to resist, and said it would be bad for them and for the city if trouble developed with the Navy. He pointed out that there were only 12 black Navy fami-lies in the whole area. The landlords subse-quently signed. There was no trouble, and the blacks were housed.

During the administration of Mayor Bill Morris, $1.6 million was spent under a block grant program to rehabilitate 571 housing units on the city's South Side, which was by then largely populated with blacks. Another $1.6 million was spent on buying and demol-ishing old buildings and relocating people, leading Morris to say in 1982 that the ghetto was disappearing.

A black businessman who has lived in Waukegan all his life agrees that in the last 10 years, blacks have moved into all sections of the city. However, he says, some of the old problems such as inflated prices, difficulties in obtaining loans, and overly large down pay-ments still plague blacks attempting to buy houses in some areas. As late as 1970, he claims, a banker showed him a map on which certain areas were outlined in red. The bank would issue a loan to a black family, but only within those areas.

Another black man, who came to North Chicago in 1941, said he was told by the mayor that he could live anywhere in that city where he could afford to buy a house. Thus, high un-employment among blacks continues to be a segregating factor in many communities.

One of those who moved north also moved right up the political ladder to become the first black mayor in Lake County. Bobby Thompson arrived in North Chicago from

Florence, Alabama, in 1957, got married, and started his own business. After serving as an alderman for six years, in 1983 he was appointed to finish the term of Mayor Leo Kukla, who had resigned due to ill health. He met almost immediate opposition from a small cadre of aldermen, who had expected him to be an uncontroversial figurehead. But Thompson's adept handling of a difficult situation led to his reelection in 1985, when he soundly defeated his opponent in the Democratic primary. (There was no Republican challenger.) His support was biracial, including one-third of the white vote.

Another Lake County politician, who was suddenly thrust into the national spotlight by events in Washington, D.C., was Robert McClory of Lake Bluff, a congressional representative from the 13th District. As a member of the judiciary committee, he was required to take a stand on the Watergate issue. McClory was a staunch Republican who had served in the House for 20 years. Nevertheless, he voted to charge Nixon with abuse of the power of his office and with refusing to respond to subpoenas.

The 1970s hit Waukegan and North Chicago hard in the pocketbook. Almost overnight, it seemed, they lost their blue-collar, big-paycheck status along with other Midwestern cities. One by one, plants closed or cut

back. U.S. Steel, which at its zenith in the 1950s employed 3,000 and was the world's largest wire-producing plant, shut its gates and laid off the last 560 employees in the fall of 1979. The old bridge over the railroad tracks, which had rung with the footsteps of thousands of men carrying lunch pails, was left empty and rusting.

Manville Corp. (formerly Johns-Manville), which also employed 3,000 in Waukegan at one time, is still involved in bankruptcy proceedings due to asbestos-related health claims, and has a work force of less than 600. Outboard Marine Corporation, with a one-time payroll of 5,000 employees, laid off 1,200 in 1983 and moved part of its operation to the Sunbelt. Today they employ less than 2,000 in Lake County. The list goes on and, according to area economists, it is not farfetched to say 20,000 people have been affected by the

heavy industry pull-out either directly or through a "ripple effect".

At the same time, new industry has emerged in the form of high-tech firms, along Routes 41 and I-94. According to the *Daily Herald*, nearly 20,000 Lake County residents are now employed in the bio-tech and health care fields. Abbott Laboratories with more than 11,000 employees and Baxter Healthcare Corporation with 13,000 lead the way.

Sleek office buildings of glass and steel and small, clean, high-tech manufacturing plants seem to rise overnight from the prairie, filling the development parks from Lincolnshire to Lake Bluff as fast as they are opened. According to an article in the *Chicago Tribune*, in the two years between November 1983 and November 1985 the number of jobs in Lake County grew by 20 percent.

With urbanization and more leisure time, new kinds of jobs also came into being. Wauconda, which was incorporated in 1877

Left: *Bobby Thompson came from Florence, Alabama, to North Chicago, and has moved from serving customers from behind a meat counter as owner of his own butcher shop, to serving constituents from behind the mayor's desk. Appointed to finish the term of ailing four-term Mayor Leo Kukla, Thompson proved not to be a mere caretaker, but took active control of the city's government. He was elected in his own right in 1987 by more than two-to-one over his party rival, and ran unopposed in the general election. Courtesy, Waukegan News-Sun*

in 1973 when the Marriott Corporation unveiled plans for a theme park on 650 acres near Gurnee. The village was quick to annex the land. Concerns of neighboring citizens were also addressed. To those who feared Gurnee would lose its rural character, Michael Kernan of the *Washington Post* said, ". . . the truth is [Gurnee] is already swamped with subdivisions that will multiply its population sevenfold before the decade is out."

The park, called Great America, opened on May 29, 1976, with all the hoopla appropriate to the nation's bicentennial. By mid-July it admitted its one-millionth visitor. In 1984 it was purchased by Bally Manufacturing Corporation, and its name was changed to Six Flags Great America.

Lake County's greatest asset has always been its waterways. Today more than ever they are being utilized for recreation to the economic benefit of the county. The market for boating has doubled every decade since World War II. In the last five years the number of boats registered to Lake County residents has jumped from 12,309 to 15,169. These figures, which represent a hefty financial outlay, do not even take into account boats registered to out-of-area residents but used on Lake County waterways.

Through the 1950s and 1960s nothing was done to maintain the Chain O'Lakes, although they were becoming increasingly polluted because of more year-round housing, greater boating activity, and widespread use of chemicals in agriculture. There were problems with algae, shallow channels making many lakes unnavigable, and increasing danger from flooding. Then in 1975 there was a big hue and cry from Lake County members of the state legislature, who were successful in making that body cough up $940,000 for dredging.

Most of the work, however, was diagnostic until 1985, when the Chain O'Lakes-Fox River Waterway Management Agency was created. They have been concerned with dredging as well as traffic on the chain.

Early settlers' hopes of making Waukegan a major shipping port never materialized, although as late as 1955 the Waukegan Port District was formed and the harbor widened and deepened to accommodate ocean-going

Above: *The landmark flag tower of Six Flags Great America can be seen for miles around its Gurnee location, attracting thousands of visitors to the theme park originally built by the Marriott Corp. Above, the flag is framed by one of the theme park's roller coasters, The Tidal Wave. Courtesy,* Waukegan News-Sun

and boasted one of three chartered academies in the county as early as 1857, was once the center of a thriving limestone industry. No one then would have guessed that someday, thousands of people would troop out to Wauconda annually to pick apples—for fun. The pick-your-own Wauconda Orchards, with 10,000 trees spread over 250 acres, has grown to include a country store, kitchen, and greenhouse. On the premises are an 1867 farmhouse and cheese factory, which are no longer in operation.

Another tourist attraction, destined to draw millions to the county, was first proposed

vessels. In 1959 the *Prinz Wilhelm George* arrived in Waukegan from the Netherlands to pick up engines from Outboard Marine. It was the first foreign ship and nearly the last. Lake craft still bring gypsum rock and cement for two lakeshore industries, but there is little other commercial activity. Even the commercial fishing industry, which once hauled millions of pounds of fish from the lake annually, has pulled in its lines.

Things looked bleak in the 1970s, when pollution closed the beaches and the harbor was found to be full of toxic polychlorinated biphenyl (PCB) from Outboard Marine dumpings. The PCB problem has yet to be solved, despite intervention by the Environmental Protection Agency. Manville Corporation, also cited by the EPA for a toxic dumpsite, was scheduled to begin cleanup in 1988.

Recreation did for Waukegan Harbor what commercialism never could, through $4 million appropriated by the state legislature in 1977. Another $8 million followed in 1981. A breakwater was built, as well as 763 boating slips in the south harbor and 284 in the north harbor. Today all of the slips are rented. By 1988 a total of $17 million had been spent on harbor expansion. An additional $36 million is anticipated to be spent for further harbor improvements to the south, which will include an additional 1,000 slips. And in Winthrop Harbor the $75-million North Point Marina, which will provide berths for 1,500 boats, is under construction.

Stocking of the lake with game fish began in the mid-1960s, and has allowed Waukegan to lay claim to its present title, "Coho

Capital of the World." The annual Coho Derby, started in 1968, draws fishermen from all over the country.

Dreamers and planners are having a heyday with the harbor developments, foreseeing Waukegan as the "Riviera of the Midwest" and Winthrop Harbor as a second Door County, Wisconsin. There is no doubt that a market exists for more restaurants, motels, convention facilities, and auxiliary tourist services, but the extent of the growth still remains to be seen.

Lake County's central waterway, the Des Plaines River, can vary from a meandering trickle to a powerful rushing torrent spilling over the floodplain. Lake County residents, to their dismay, learned this firsthand in the

Above: Beginning with the devastating "100-year flood" that struck the county in the fall, the years 1986-1987 were not kind to the Rustic Manor, a popular, long-time restaurant in Gurnee. The restaurant, first ruined by several feet of water that overflowed from the nearby Des Plaines River, was then destroyed by fire in the summer of 1987. It has not yet been rebuilt, owing to changes in the state law made to prevent recurrences of flood damage. Photo by Mary Carmody

(Left: Housing was a critical problem for soldiers and sailors returning to Lake County after World War II. Their first housing project to be built under the jurisdiction of the Lake County Housing Authority was the Marion Jones Project in North Chicago, which opened in 1964, nearly 20 years after the war's end, and 18 years after the Authority was created. Courtesy Waukegan News-Sun

Facing page: *Sunrise at the Waukegan Harbor finds a solitary fisherman making preparations for his day's labors on Lake Michigan. The bare masts of the moored sailboats rise like tapers in the dawn sky. Photo by Mary Carmody*

fall of 1986 when large sections of Gurnee and communities to the south were innundated with water. They knew that the Des Plaines had flooded before, but in between people tend to forget, and the amount of building that had been done in the floodplain since the last flood led to damage running into the millions of dollars in 1986.

The county board had learned its lesson back in the 1950s and banned building in the floodplain, but has no jurisdiction over municipalities which allow it. But since the fall of 1986, people have been treading a little more cautiously and many studies are underway, including one by the U.S. Corps of Engineers.

Kernan of the *Washington Post* was right on target about the growth of Gurnee. In the decade between 1976 and 1986, the town leaped from 4,000 residents to almost 10,000. According to an article in the *Chicago Tribune,* 2,000 housing units were under construction in January 1988. Their occupancy brings the population to about 14,000—a figure that is expected to rise to 20,000 by the year 2000.

The growth in Buffalo Grove (which straddles the Lake-Cook County line), Lake Zurich, and Vernon Hills has been equally dramatic. Million-dollar homes have been built from Riverwoods and Barrington Hills on the south to near Wadsworth on the north. Waterfront lots all along the chain are selling for premium prices.

In 1980 the population of Lake County was 440,372—an increase of 15 percent in 10 years. The median age was 28, and 25 percent had college degrees. Results of a survey published by *Sales Marketing and Management* magazine in October 1986 showed the average, effective buying-power per household to be $36,405, placing Lake County seventh among U.S. metro areas. Figures published recently by *The News-Sun* ranked the county as the second richest in northeastern Illinois, with a per capita income of $15,292.

Yet there is also great poverty, not only in the industrialized cities along the Lake Michigan shoreline but in rural settings as well. Hainesville reported that 15.5 percent of its residents were below the poverty level in the 1980 census, and in Highwood, surrounded by great wealth, 7.5 percent live below the pov-

erty level. Agencies, churches, and individuals have risen to the challenge of helping the poor: Catholic Charities of Lake County, the Chaplaincy Service, a number of food pantries and soup kitchens, and the Lake County Coalition for the Homeless all have made great strides. United Way of Lake County, which funds 96 programs through 35 agencies, raised $3.7 million in 1987—70 percent of it from individual contributions. Loretta Schwartz-Nobel, author of *Starving in the Shadow of Plenty,* said in 1981, ". . . it is clear that the need is great and that the city of Chicago has done more toward meeting it than many other cities." This could apply to the entire Chicago area, including Lake County.

After the rash of incorporations in the 1950s, there were only four between 1960 and 1988. They were: Green Oaks and Mettawa in 1960, Wadsworth in 1962, and Tower Lakes in 1966. Green Oaks slipped in under the wire, much to the consternation of Libertyville. Green Oaks filed for incorporation on December 30, 1959, and on January 1, 1960, a new law took effect requiring the minimum population for incorporation to be 400 instead of 100. Green Oaks had 200. Libertyville protested, had its day in court, and lost.

Lake County's 47th and newest community is Beach Park, which voted for incorporation on March 15, 1988. Located between Waukegan and Zion, and nearly surrounding the Waukegan Memorial Airport, it was opposed by both communities. Winning the vote by a ratio of two to one, Beach Park's 11,000 inhabitants chose to govern themselves.

Where there were 173,100 acres of farmland in 1950, there were only 92,135 in 1982. The battle between open-space advocates, led by county board member F.T. "Mike" Graham, and developers rages hot in Lake County. It has been projected that by the year 2005 there will remain only 86,860 acres of undeveloped land, which includes agriculture and natural resources but not lakes and rivers. Those remain our unchanging open space: 16,780 acres.

While the county grows, the county also seriously preserves its history, following a national ground swell of support in the 1970s. On May 3, 1978, after months of research by members of the Waukegan Historical Society,

Left: *A solid freeze on the Chain O'Lakes will transform a frozen landscape into a bustling scene as ice fishermen set up their plastic wind shields and try their luck. Since formation of the Chain O'Lakes Fox River Waterway Management Agency in 1985, a coordinated effort to clean out and improve the lakes has added to their ever-growing popularity for summer—and winter—sports. Photo by Thomas Delany, Jr.*

Right: *They didn't get away! Charter-boat fishing has become a major recreational and business endeavor on Lake Michigan. The lake was stocked with game fish beginning in the mid-1960s, and Waukegan now claims title as the "Coho Salmon Capital of the World," conducting a Coho Derby every summer to prove it. A $17-million harbor expansion program, started in 1977, added more than 1,000 boating slips, all rented, and further additions are planned. Photo by Mary Carmody*

Left: *Spectators give a cheer as the winner of the Lake County Marathon approaches the finish line in Ravinia Park. Photo by Mary Carmody*

Below Left: *The Chicago Bears are number one to many in Lake County. Photo by Mary Carmody*

Below: *The Lake County Marathon attracts up to 800 runners each year. Photo by Mary Carmody*

Parades abound during the summer months in Lake County, and Zion's annual Jubilee Days Parade on Labor Day attracts numbers in the thousands. Once the largest parade of its kind in Illinois, the festivities attracted viewers from nearby Wisconsin and not-so-near Indiana, as well as the Chicago-metropolitan area. The various parade units of the Shriners, including their dancing Indian, above, are usually included. Photo by Mary Carmody

Above: *A violinist from a mariachi band pauses for a picture at Waukegan's annual Lakefront Ethnic Festival, held each summer along Lake Michigan's beach. Photo by Mary Carmody*

Left: *Waukegan celebrates its ethnic diversity during its annual Fourth of July Parade. The sign on the approaching float, "Nationalities from Around the World" is no idle boast, and the city's people include Hispanics, Africans, Orientals, Asians, Polish, Croatians, Slovenians, Serbians, Lithuanians, Armenians, Irish, to name a few. Photo by Mary Carmody*

Agriculture continues to play a role in Lake County, although it is diminishing as housing developments spring up where corn and soybeans used to grow. Especially popular among tourists are the area's orchards and fruit farms, where apple picking abounds in early fall, and pumpkins beckon as Halloween approaches. And those are no small pumpkins! Photo by Mary Carmody

Right: *The revival of the Market Day in Libertyville each Thursday during the summer and early fall has been well-received by vendors and patrons alike. Trucks line the street around Cook Memorial Park, farmers display their fresh fruits, vegetables, and flowers, and the historical Cook mansion and rose garden stand behind. Photo by Mary Carmody*

Above: *Christmas lights along Lake Forest's Market Square beckon shoppers and browsers from throughout the county and from Chicago and its suburbs. Market Square's appeal has yet to succumb to the lure of area shopping centers, and Lake Forest retains a viable downtown shopping environment. Photo by Mary Carmody*

Right: *The popularity of the Lake County Fair has continued since formation of the Lake County Agricultural Society in 1851. Held each mid-summer on the specially constructed fairgrounds in Grayslake, the fair attracts young and old exhibitors alike, including this charmer who is obviously appreciated by her pet goats. Photo by Mary Carmody*

the city's Near North Historic District was placed on the National Register of Historic Places by the Department of Conservation. Of the 449 structures in the district, 68 were highlighted as possessing special architectural and/or historical significance. According to the department report key landmarks are the focal points, but background buildings help to unify the entire streetscape.

Among the buildings is the ornate Genesee Theater, which opened on Christmas Day 1927 billed as the "Wonder Theater of the North Shore." After serving thousands of moviegoers for decades, it fell into decline. It was finally rescued in 1980 by a nonprofit community group, Friends of the Historic Genesee, which sponsors live theater and concerts.

Shimer College, which began in Mt. Carroll, Illinois, moved to Waukegan in 1979 and set up school in a historic district Italianate house, which had been built before the college was founded in 1853. A small liberal arts school with a curriculum based on the great books of the western world, it has prospered in Waukegan—growing from 40 students to over 100 in 1988. In 1988 Shimer expanded its campus to include a 1917 home recently occupied by the YWCA, a coachhouse, and two other buildings. Their goal is to acquire the entire block, and restore the buildings in keeping with the historic character of the area.

The 1847 classic white house at 414 North Sheridan, deemed "one of the finest examples of the Greek revival style in Illinois," was purchased by the Waukegan/Lake County Chamber Foundation (an educational foundation) for the offices of the Waukegan/Lake County Chamber of Commerce in 1981. This follows a trend in downtown Waukegan, where beautiful old homes have been renovated by lawyers for use as offices and stand in sharp contrast to the modern county buildings complex.

Communities throughout the county have worked to preserve their heritage. In Wadsworth, the old one-room Wadsworth School was turned into the village hall. During the bicentennial year Antioch residents recreated the Hiram Buttrick Sawmill on Sequoit Creek, on the site chosen by the first settlers, Darius and Thomas Gage. The Zion

Historical Society acquired John Dowie's home, and is renovating it as a museum and depository for his copious writings.

The imposing mansion built in 1878 in downtown Libertyville by Ansel B. Cook, Illinois legislator, Chicago alderman, and Lake County teacher, was willed to the village for use as a library. When the library outgrew the premises, a modern building was annexed to the mansion. It is now maintained as a Victorian home museum by the Libertyville-Mundelein Historical Society.

Long Grove, settled by German farmers at the crossing of two Indian trails in the 1830s, epitomizes the lure of the historic and the antique. Major roads were routed around the village, and it was left to its sleepy existence. It was not until after World War II that someone opened an antique shop, and one led to another. Today thousands of people annually come to Long Grove to shop, browse, and eat at the almost 100 specialty shops and restaurants. Many buildings are dressed up with antique-looking facades, but 17 are originals. Two are the Village Tavern, which dates back 130 years, and the Long Grove Church, which was founded in 1846. To add to the decor, the village replaced an old bridge with a covered bridge in 1972.

Despite the commercialization, Long Grove fights, often in court, to retain its rural character. Through annexations, about which its neighbors have had some unkind things to say, Long Grove has grown to 17 square miles. Yet its population remains at 2,000.

Lake County shopping patterns changed drastically beginning in the 1970s. For years, fashionable women bought their clothes at Heins in Waukegan; people in Grayslake and surrounding farms traded at Battershall's General Store; and summer folks as well as locals sipped ice cream sodas at King's Drug Store in Antioch. All were downtown. Then almost overnight, it seemed, people deserted the downtowns for the newly popular shopping centers.

Lakehurst, Lake County's first regional shopping center, opened on August 19, 1971. Located on the former Thomas Wilson farm, the land had been annexed by Waukegan through a special agreement with Park City. Three years later Hawthorn Center, part of a

Facing page: Fall leaves color the roadways of Lake County, especially along the Des Plaines River and in the Chain O'Lakes State Park in the northwestern corner of the county. Nature's beauty abounds in the county's numerous forest preserves, many of which are adjacent to the Des Plaines River, making public use of land in flood plain areas that is unsuitable for other building. Photo by Mary Carmody

sprawling development called New Century Town, opened its doors. It was on the site of the Joseph Medill Patterson estate, which had been bought by millionaire John Cuneo. The developer approached Libertyville concerning annexation early in the planning, but a vociferous faction in the village opposed it. Instead of going away the developer simply turned to Vernon Hills on the other side, which eagerly jumped at the chance to annex—and thereby reap untold tax benefits.

Faced with declining, decaying downtowns, communities reacted in various ways, but none more dramatically than Highland Park, which did not choose to do its facelift "one wrinkle at a time" according to *News-*

Above: *The Zion Passion Play celebrated its 50th anniversary year of performances in 1985. The religious pageant involves more than 2,500 cast, crew and chorus members. Courtesy* The News-Sun

Right: *Guide Barbara McMahon talks to school children inside the Ott Log cabin in Deerfield, where a family of nine lived in the single room and loft. The cabin, owned by one of Deerfield's first settlers, has been restored. Courtesy* The News-Sun

Sun reporter Doug Weatherwax. Through a joint effort by the city and private developers the two-block Port Clinton Square, in the heart of Highland Park, opened in 1984. It includes office and retail space, a parking garage, a streetscape extending beyond the center, and a decorative arch.

These new shopping malls often are the setting for concerts and art exhibits, playing the traditional role formerly performed by town squares and demonstrating the continuing importance of culture in Lake County. Waukegan, Lake Forest, and Highland Park each have symphony orchestras. In Zion there is a chamber orchestra and the Passion Play, which draws thousands each year. Palette, Masque and Lyre in Antioch and the Bowen Park Opera Company in Waukegan offer live theater, as do dozens of other community groups. The Lake County Art League and the Lake County Watercolor Guild hold exhibits regularly. And groups like the American-Croatian Waukegan Tamburitizans preserve the ethnic culture.

Music has been the spice of life for Lake Countians since the first settlers came up the Des Plaines, bringing with them tunes like "Turkey in the Straw." In the bad times they sang "When Johnny Comes Marching Home" and "Where Have All The Flowers Gone"; in the good they danced the Charleston and rock 'n' rolled. They have expressed themselves with polkas and mariachi bands and hard rock. Now as they mark time, observing the 150th anniversary of the county, they are proud of those who have led the march to this point and confident that this rich and vital land will continue to provide a snug harbor for its citizens.

Brick paths lead shoppers through the main street of Long Grove, where antique shops and other specialty stores attract thousands of visitors each year. Courtesy The News-Sun

Right: *In a letter to J. Hill at "The Fair" in Chicago in the summer of 1908, a Mr. Kirby, staying in Fox Lake, described life as "pretty soft out here." At Emil Jahnke's Resort in Fox Lake, "Berghoff Beer" was on draught and ice cream cones were a nickel in Emil's Annex. Courtesy, Lake County Museum*

CHAPTER 7

PARTNERS IN PROGRESS

From Lake-Cook Road to the south, the Wisconsin border to the north, Lake Michigan to the east, and McHenry County to the west, Lake County is booming.

According to the Illinois Department of Economic Security, Lake County has added 9,500 new jobs since 1984. Most of them have been in small businesses. This growth is clear evidence that the entrepreneurial experience is alive and well in the county. Its population is now roughly 500,000. Between 1980 and 1986 the number of employers in Lake County increased from 7,500 to 10,000, and most of that growth—1,600 of the new employers—was firms employing from one to four people.

Among the reasons for such growth is plenty of open land, excellent transportation, and a growing and well-educated labor force. Low taxes are an attractive lure for many firms.

While Lake Zurich is the fastest-growing town in the county, with nearby Wauconda not far behind, growth is especially explosive along Lake-Cook Road, the Tri-State Tollway, and Milwaukee Road Illinois Highway 21).

Housing is developing at a rapid pace, and within the past few years office space has doubled in the North Corridor from 6.6 million square feet to more than 13 million.

Rapid retail growth is also reaching westward along Illinois Highway 60 through Vernon Hills and Mundelein. The shopping space in this corridor has doubled in recent years to surpass 2 million square feet. Hawthorne Center was the regional mall that opened 15 years ago and put Vernon Hills on the map.

Corporate headquarters are finding Lake County a congenial place; the largest newcomer to date is Sears Consumer Financial Corporation's Discover Card with a 6-million-square-foot home.

Health-related companies remain the dominant force in the area, employing more than 15,000 people.

It is within this setting that the businesses and public service institutions profiled in the following chapter operate. While they offer a wide variety of products and services in the Lake County area, each one of them approaches its customers or clients with the same frame of mind. In all cases, they are adept at anticipating and than satisfying their customers' needs. They understand the advantages of the latest technologies and how to adapt them to their businesses. They do not fear competition; rather, they welcome it. Without exception, they are proud of their role as Lake County employers, and every firm profiled can cite a high number of long-term employees. Many of these businesses provide summer jobs for local youths. The companies are also civic-minded and participate actively in local service organizations.

In sum, the Partners in Progress exemplify the best in American business. They are entrepreneurial as well as enlightened. Some still reflect the powerful individuality of their founders. The larger, older ones that have become huge corporations nevertheless still remember their roots. These organizations, whose stories are detailed on the following pages, have chosen to support this important literary and civic project. They illustrate the variety of ways in which individuals and their businesses have contributed to the area's growth and development. All know that the past points to the future. And it is a future that they believe is bright with promise—both for themselves and for Lake County.

WAUKEGAN/LAKE COUNTY CHAMBER OF COMMERCE

The Waukegan/Lake County Chamber of Commerce is a volunteer organization of business people in the Waukegan/Lake County area. It was chartered in 1915 as the Waukegan Commercial Association; in 1917 it was renamed the Waukegan Chamber of Commerce. It was known as the Waukegan-North Chicago Chamber of Commerce and then as the Waukegan-North Chicago Area Chamber of Commerce. The organization assumed its present name in 1975.

The purpose of the chamber has always been to increase economic activity in the Waukegan/Lake County economic area. It is led by an elected board of directors of 18 businesspeople from throughout Lake County. Represented are small business firms, commercial store owners, professionals, and manufacturers. The chamber has more than 600 employer/members.

Committees or task forces of interested members carry on the chamber's work, which centers on three areas:

Economic development includes seeking to help new businesses relocate in Lake County as well as nurturing existing firms. The chamber also holds seminars on foreign trade, promotes tourism development, and holds discussions on industrial relations.

Under community and county development, the chamber provides an economic data base, supports quality education for all Lake County residents, seeks adequate transportation throughout the county, works to ensure high environmental quality, and helps develop reasonable and just zoning and annexation ordinances.

The governmental affairs division involves chamber members in legislative and tax issues on the state, national, and local levels.

The chamber has played a major role in the successful development of a variety of projects in the Waukegan/Lake County area. Among them are the formation of the College of Lake County Community College District,

The chamber's renovated headquarters building, known as The Little White House, is a designated historic structure and a rare example of a one-story Greek revival building.

the establishment of the Lake County, Illinois, Convention and Visitors' Bureau, and the creation of the Waukegan Port District.

The chamber has been active in school district consolidations; home rule government for Lake County; a career guidance consortium; a youth conservation corps; Forward Luncheons, begun almost 60 years ago as public affairs forums to enhance understanding of business-related economic needs; the Business Resource Library at the chamber headquarters with various resource volumes and periodicals that pertain to business; an associate office of the U.S. Department of Commerce and Small Business Administration Resource Center; Management Development Seminars, which examine problems of mutual interest about management; a Major Employers' Field Day, the annual golf outing for chamber members and their guests; and the Ambassador Club, an elite group of retired chamber members who continue to serve as the public relations and good will arm of the chamber.

An important auxiliary arm of the chamber is the Waukegan/Lake County Chamber Foundation, which informs, as well as encourages, the public that it is possible to acquire historic structures and to rehabilitate them for

meaningful purposes. The chamber's renovated headquarters building is a designated historic structure and a rare example of a one-story Greek revival building.

The Waukegan/Lake County Chamber of Commerce works diligently to maintain its national accreditation by the Chamber of Commerce of the United States.

The original charter issued on March 5, 1915, for the Waukegan Commercial Association later to become the Waukegan/Lake County Chamber of Commerce.

NORTH SHORE SAVINGS AND LOAN ASSOCIATION

The North Shore Savings and Loan Association, founded in 1921, is a mutual association that provides a full range of financial services—savings, investments, home mortgages—to its customers. North Shore Savings has assets of more than $150 million.

The association was founded after a group of civic-minded citizens found they all shared the problem of home financing. They petitioned for approval from the state auditor on April 4, 1921, to organize a building and loan association. Some three weeks later an organization meeting was called with 57 prospective stockholders present. Bylaws were presented and adopted, and a board of directors was named. To this day members of the board and employees of the association are local individuals who live in Waukegan or nearby.

Chartered on May 2, 1921, with original capitalization of one million dollars, North Shore Building and Loan Association was officially in existence. On May 7, 1921, the first day of operation, $106.25 was collected in weekly dues and $106.25 was paid in membership fees. The first application for a home loan was received on May 19, 1921, and approved two weeks later for $500.

At the end of the first full year of operation the association had assets of $16,096.18, with 1,017 shares in force.

In 1923 the federal government created the Federal Home Loan Bank to help savings and loan associations nationwide weather the Depression. North Shore applied and received membership certificate No. 13 on January 3, 1933; between February 4 and April 29, 1933, the association borrowed $43,200 from the Federal Home Loan Bank primarily to meet withdrawal demands.

On June 9, 1936, the board passed a resolution that the building owned by the association at 11th and Park in North Chicago be remodeled for its new office. Dedication was held September 20, 1936. There was now a small lobby, a private office for interviews, and a larger main office containing two tellers' windows.

At the end of World War II the directors realized that a building boom

---

The North Shore Savings and Loan Association, at 700 South Lewis Avenue, was chartered on May 2, 1921, primarily to provide home loans. Today it provides a full range of financial services.

was imminent, and they wanted North Shore Savings to play a part in it. The board decided to move the association to a more prominent location, and in the spring of 1950 it moved to a new building in the heart of the 10th Street business district. The asset base was $3.6 million, and the name of the association was changed to its present one.

By the end of the 1960s assets had mounted to $12 million. An expensive remodeling program provided seven teller windows, a walking window, and five offices. The directors realized that, even after remodeling, the 10th Street building would soon be obsolete.

In 1968 the board purchased the site of the association's present location on South Lewis Avenue. After careful planning, construction started in the fall of 1970, and the association opened for business in its new, 30,000-square-foot facility on December 13, 1971. There is parking available for 100 cars.

Looking to the future, North Shore Savings and Loan Association plans to continue to emphasize its tradition of friendly professional service. It has expanded its present range of services to include the introduction of a financial planning service, and the marketing of mutual funds and tax-deferred annuities.

VICTORY MEMORIAL HOSPITAL

Victory Memorial Hospital is a fully accredited, not-for-profit community hospital licensed for 406 acute care beds. Located adjacent to Waukegan's Victory Park, many of the hospital's rooms and sunporches overlook magnificent Lake Michigan and have a view of Waukegan's spires and skyline.

Victory also operates the Victory Immediate Care Center in Gurnee, and the Victory Lakes Continuing Care Center in Lindenhurst for those in need of skilled geriatric care. The hospital has an affiliation with the YMCA to provide adult day-care services and a wellness program. Victory is dedicated to providing high-quality, compassionate patient care, education for health professionals, and community service.

Quality through teamwork is its mandate. Victory's dedicated and highly qualified team consists of physicians, nurses, volunteers, therapists, technicians, dietitians, housekeepers, engineers, and many others. The physicians diagnose and prescribe treatment; the nurses and technicians directly administer care; dedicated volunteers provide an understanding ear; and the others provide support services.

The hospital offers comprehensive medical and surgical services, including 24-hour emergency room services, family-centered maternity care, industrial medical services, chemical dependency treatment, one-day surgery, cardiac rehabilitation, oncology care, special services for older adults, home health care, medical and surgical critical care, outpatient and inpatient renal dialysis, telemetry (heart rhythm monitoring), and pastoral care. In addition, there is an adolescent chemical dependency unit, the only one of its kind located in and serving northern and western Lake County, and the North Lake County MRI, which offers the latest technological developments in magnetic resonance imaging.

Victory Hospital continually updates and acquires state-of-the-art technology, such as a computed tomo-

Construction began on the present site of Victory Memorial Hospital in the early 1920s. The hospital was dedicated as a memorial to those who served in World War I.

graphic whole body scanner, digital subtraction angiography, and microfocus mammography. These and other sophisticated systems offer the latest advances for determining diagnoses and treatments.

The hospital has nine operating suites—the largest number of any hospital in Lake County—as well as the largest kidney dialysis program in the county. Victory Hospital is also Lake County's designated facility for treating injured patients who have been exposed to radioactivity. A separate radiation containment room is located adjacent to the hospital's emergency department. Specially trained physicians and nurses manage these cases.

There are more than 1,000 employees dedicated to restoring patients to better health. Each patient is assigned a primary nurse, responsible for planning, coordinating, and evaluating the patient's nursing care for all shifts. Patients can rely on this nurse for explaining procedures and answering questions.

Nursing staff members receive ed-ucation beyond basic nursing. Geriatrics, oncology, and critical care courses are regularly offered to update them in the latest concepts for application to their work.

More than 400 dedicated men and women donate 41,000 hours of service to the hospital each year. These volunteers deliver mail, flowers, and newspapers; manage the gift shop; make friendly visits to patients; play with pediatric patients; deliver medications from the pharmacy; and perform many other services. Victory's Auxiliary acts as a fund-raising arm. Funds donated to Victory by the auxiliary come from the gift shop, bake sales, book sales, auctions, brunches, and the uniform shop.

Victory's industrial medical services provide specially designed on-site health screenings, physical examinations, and employee education programs customized for industrial clients. Immediate benefits to employers include quick reporting on an employee's health status and rapid return to the job. The screening and educational components of the industrial service program encourage employees to engage in better health practices. Longer-term benefits include a reduction in health care costs, plus an overall improvement in employee morale.

For the community at large, Victory offers a wide range of screenings, health education, and support programs—first aid courses; blood pressure, skin cancer, diabetes, and other health screenings; courses in caring for the aged at home; instruction in breast self-examination; and many more. Childbirth education classes, stop smoking courses, Alcoholics Anonymous groups, CPR training, and seminars in stress management and coping with grief are among the courses open to the public. Members of the hospital's Speakers Bureau address community groups and clubs on a broad spectrum of subjects ranging from how to manage arthritis to how to control the costs of medical care. Victory Lakes Continuing Care Center in Lindenhurst provides health education, screening, adult day-care services, and other programs for the entire community.

Victory offers continuing professional education for physicians, nurses, and other health care professionals. The hospital sponsors a school for respiratory therapy technician training, programs for radiologic technicians, and a wide range of nursing courses. Victory physicians are regularly addressed by eminent medical specialists.

Victory Memorial Hospital traces its beginning to 1891, when its predecessor, The Lake County Hospital, became the first hospital chartered in Lake County. Construction began on the present site in the early 1920s, when the hospital was dedicated as a memorial to those who served in World War I.

The present building was constructed in phases during the years between 1950 and 1985. The latest addition is an innovative one-day surgery facility.

Victory's New Family Center offers parents the choice of delivering their baby in an LDRP (labor, delivery, recovery, postpartum) setting or in the traditional labor, delivery, and recov-

ery facilities. The completely remodeled maternity wing includes the latest technical equipment, birthing beds, an expanded nursery, and even a children's playroom for siblings. Numerous childbirth education classes, including Lamaze, are offered throughout the year.

All residents of Lake County are eligible to join the Victory Memorial Hospital Association, which elects nine of the 20-member hospital governing board, responsible for directing all hos-

Adjacent to Victory Park and overlooking Lake Michigan, Victory Memorial Hospital is dedicated to providing high-quality, compassionate patient care, education for health professionals, and community service.

pital policy issues and for overseeing the financial resources of the institution. Other members of the board are appointed by community organizations.

Victory Memorial Hospital is licensed by the City of Waukegan, the Illinois Department of Public Health, and the U.S. Department of Health, Education, and Welfare. It is fully accredited by the Joint Commission on the Accreditation of Hospitals.

The hospital's services, staff, and programs are sensitive to the needs of its patients, their families, and their friends. Victory offers care delivered with respect and concern. That is why the hospital believes "Our Victory Is Yours."

FANSTEEL

Fansteel is an integrated producer of refractory metals, and the firm also fabricates precision metal products. The company classifies its products into three business segments: metal products, industrial tools, and metal fabrications.

Fansteel serves a broad cross section of markets with products manufactured from a variety of materials. Most of these materials have characteristics that are unique and require manufacturing skills that are highly specialized. Processes range from the extraction of elemental material from ore through the fabrication of finished products.

The range of principal markets served spans electronics, aircraft/aerospace, weapons systems, metalworking, energy, and automotive. This diversification has served Fansteel well, as individual market cycles have tended to counterbalance one another. A planned shift of relative importance to the company has taken place with aircraft/aerospace and weapons systems accounting for 45 percent of total sales in

recent years. This is up from 36 percent in 1985 and only 25 percent in 1984. The change has been accomplished through both internal development and acquisition.

The fundamental changes occurring within Fansteel reflect the global nature of most markets and the need to establish a manufacturing presence outside the United States to remain competitive and build market share.

Interturbine-Fansteel B.V., a joint venture undertaken to serve the European (NATO) aircraft industry, was an initial step in adapting to the evolution of international markets. A second joint venture with the V Tech Corporation was established to manufacture tantalum products in Japan. V Tech-Fansteel, Inc. (majority owned by Fansteel), is fully operational with high-capacitance tantalum powders.

Fansteel manufacturing operations are performed in 13 plants nationwide.

The firm got its start in January 1907, when Carl A. Pfanstiehl and his partner, James Troxel, organized Pfanstiehl Electrical Laboratories to manufacture electrical coils that Pfanstiehl had invented. The venture was incorporated under the laws of the State of Illi-

Carl A. Pfanstiehl (shown here) and his partner, James Troxel, organized Pfanstiehl Electrical Laboratories in 1907.

nois with an initial authorized issue of capital stock of $10,000. Troxel put his $2,500 life savings into the enterprise.

Pfanstiehl was an inventive genius, a talent apparent even in his childhood in Highland Park. While still attending high school, he constructed the first X-ray machine on the Chicago North Shore. Young Pfanstiehl was frequently called from his classes to operate the machine at various hospitals.

Pfanstiehl left high school at age 16 to attend Armour Institute of Technology in Chicago (now the Illinois Institute of Technology). It was then that he and Troxel organized Pfanstiehl Electric Laboratories. Pfanstiehl produced a revolutionary induction coil in which the secondary circuit consisted of a series of pancake windings so arranged that it was virtually impossible to burn them out.

Troxel saw that the new automobiles required Pfanstiehl ignition coils. Though not a monetary success, the company gained a reputation in the automotive field; in the years before

The entire staff in 1910.

World War I, magnetoes, master vibrators, starter coils, and transformer coils were added to the automotive products line. The firm tried other ventures as well, including radios. It was not until the mid-1930s, however, that Fansteel—it changed its name to the phonetic spelling in 1918—became "an industrial company serving industry."

The 1930s was the decade in which the potential for tantalum as a chemical-processing material—a potential that had originally motivated chief researcher Clarence Balke and Carl Pfanstiehl as early as 1916—was realized. From that period Fansteel's development followed the course leading to today's position as a preeminent supplier of tantalum, columbium (niobium), and their alloys.

Fansteel's metal fabrications segment is comprised of California Drop Forge, Los Angeles; Escast, Addison, Illinois, and Sarasota, Florida; PSM, Los Angeles; Washington Manufacturing, Washington, Iowa; and Wellman Dynamics, Creston, Iowa. Most sales to the aircraft/aerospace and weapons markets are from this segment and are associated with the activities of the California Drop Forge, PSM, and Wellman Dynamics plants.

California Drop Forge produces closed die forgings of steel, titanium, and high-temperature superalloys used in both structural and rotating applications.

PSM makes metal fabrications for turbine engine and space propulsion systems and similar high-technology structures for both commercial and government markets. PSM also designs, manufactures, and qualifies flight-weight pressurized tankage and systems for propellant management on launch vehicles, space-orbiting vehicles, and the upper stages of ballistic missiles.

Wellman Dynamics manufactures high-strength and high-integrity aluminum and magnesium sand castings for aircraft, missile, and helicopter applications.

The metal products segment includes extraction and consolidation facilities in Muskogee, Oklahoma, and a mill and fabricated products plant, for tantalum and columbium, in North Chicago.

Raw materials feedstock, such as tin slags, beneficiated concentrates, natural ores, and/or scrap, are processed to products including compounds, ingot bar, powder, rod, wire, sheet, foil, tubing, and fabricated components. Principal uses for these prod-

The Fansteel complex in 1929.

ucts are found in electronic capacitors, chemical and petrochemical-processing equipment, aircraft/aerospace applications, weapons systems, nuclear hardware, and metal alloys. By far the most important in terms of sales volume is the use of tantalum in capacitors.

The industrial tools segment includes plants in Plantsville, Connecticut; Lexington, Kentucky; Beckley, West Virginia; Latrobe, Pennsylvania; and Gulfport, Mississippi.

VR/Wesson-Plantsville is a primary manufacturer of cemented tungsten carbide tools for the metalworking industry. Products include standard and special inserts, tools and blades, blanks and rounds, turning tools, milling cutters, and toolholders. A major portion of Plantsville sales is to the gas turbine segment of the aircraft/aerospace industry. VR/Wesson-Lexington makes tungsten carbide products, accessories, and supplies for the mining and construction industries. VR/Wesson-Hydro Carbide manufactures tungsten carbide products in both its Latrobe and Gulfport plants for use in wear applications, principally for metal forming and oil and gas drilling. VR/Wesson also manufactures a proprietary cast alloy known as Tantung®, used largely by the woodworking industry.

GOELITZ CONFECTIONERY COMPANY

The A&G Goelitz Confectionery Company in Belleville, Illinois, was sold by Albert and Gustav Goelitz around 1893.

It took President Ronald Reagan to introduce all of America to Jelly Belly® jelly beans, but it takes the Goelitz Confectionery Company of North Chicago and the Herman Goelitz Candy Company, Inc., of Fairfield, California, to keep Ronald Reagan's—and America's—appetites for these delicious confections satisfied.

Jelly Belly jelly beans changed the very definition of a jelly bean by flavoring the center and the shell with unusual flavors. They are smaller and more flavorful than ordinary jelly beans, which have no flavoring or color in the center.

Goelitz Confectionery is an affiliate of the Herman Goelitz Candy Company. The two firms manufacture Jelly Belly jelly beans and a wide range of Goelitz Confections® gourmet candy in the United States.

The Goelitz family has been active in the candy-making industry in the United States for well in excess of 100 years. In 1869 brothers Albert and Gustav Goelitz, recent immigrants from Germany, began making candy in a factory in Belleville, Illinois. While Gustav supervised the candy making,

Albert traveled throughout Illinois and Missouri selling from the back of a horse-drawn wagon.

As the century turned, Gustav's sons, Adolph, Herman, and Gustav Jr., and son-in-law, Edward F. Kelley, went into candy making and ran the firm known today as the Goelitz Confectionery Company. The firm specialized in butter cremes, claiming to

Edward F. Kelley (left) with Herman Goelitz circa 1920.

be the "King of the Candy Corn Field."

The business prospered, and in 1914 a new plant was built on Morrow Avenue in North Chicago where today the company continues to make candy. In those 74 years two more generations of Goelitz and Kelley family members carried on the tradition, running the business through good times and bad. Their expertise and contribution has had a major impact on the confectionery industry in the United States.

The seeds were planted for a tremendous growth in business when the California branch of the family, under the Herman Goelitz, Inc., flagship, accepted a request from a California entrepreneur to make a jelly bean with "natural" flavors. The firm eventually purchased the rights to this new bean: Universal notoriety was to descend upon the company.

In 1978 Herman Rowland, president of Herman Goelitz, Inc., and his cousin, William Kelley, Jr., grandson of one of the original founders, Ed Kelley, consolidated the Goelitz name into a single, national gourmet brand of confections. The product lines were increased, Jelly Belly beans were given greater distribution, and Candy Corn

production continued.

California Governor Ronald Reagan had begun to eat jelly beans supplied to him by the California company to help him quit smoking. When Jelly Belly beans were introduced in 1976, he became a fan. Four years later the candy company was asked to supply Jelly Belly jelly beans at the Republican Party's national convention in Detroit. During the convention *Time* magazine ran a photograph of the Reagan family enjoying a big jar of jelly beans. The national press followed the story and besieged the firm for stories and photos.

Soon Jelly Belly jelly beans were at Camp David, on *Air Force One,* at the White House, and on the space shuttle *Challenger.* News photographs of cabinet meetings showed a large cut-glass jar of the famous jelly beans on the middle of the table. Other photos showed the secretaries of defense and treasury with Jelly Belly jelly beans. Word from Blair House, the official guest house for foreign dignitaries, was that visiting kings, presidents, and prime ministers were requesting President Reagan's favorite confection.

Round-the-clock shifts, both in California and in North Chicago, were ordered to meet the demand. Plant operations had to be expanded, new equipment installed, and more em-

---

Candy makers in the North Chicago factory circa 1915. The barrels in the foreground contain corn syrup.

ployees hired. In 1985 a new 100,000-square-foot production facility, warehouse, and corporate headquarters was constructed in Fairfield, California, to increase production five times over.

Today Herman Goelitz, Inc., and Goelitz Confectionery Company, make 40 flavors of Jelly Belly jelly beans and more than 100 gourmet candies, including Candy Corn, Peppermint Wafers, Dutch Mints®, Wiggle Worms®, Jordan Almonds, and Licorice Pastels.

While Jelly Belly jelly beans are the most well-known product offered, Goelitz Confectionery Company is an aggressive competitor, introducing new candies using state-of-the-art manufacturing equipment, and selling to fine stores throughout the United States and around the world.

THE TRAVELODGE

Ever since it was officially opened by Mayor Robert Sabonjian in 1964, The Travelodge, at 222 Grand Avenue in Waukegan, has been the central place to stay.

Host and co-owner Jim Stiles offers 62 clean, comfortable, single- and double-bed rooms with complimentary coffee, direct-dial telephones, large color television sets, and reasonable rates.

Conveniently located on the north edge of downtown Waukegan, within walking distance of the harbor marina, train station, shopping district, Lake County Courthouse, Greyhound Bus station, theaters, and restaurants, The Travelodge has been a visible landmark in Waukegan for years. It is sited on the southern end of the city's Historic District.

Businessmen appreciate its proximity to Outboard Marine, Manville, and Abbott Laboratories. Travelodge guests also like the availability of small meeting rooms and special rates. A coffee shop is on the premises, and there is an ice machine on every floor. There is also an outdoor, heated swimming pool.

Because Travelodge is part of the Trust House-Forte Group, a British company, the Waukegan Travelodge has a good number of foreign guests every year. By using a toll-free number, guests may make reservations at Travelodges and Viscount Hotels in the United States and Canada.

Travelodge is also the official information and translation facility in America for the United States Travel Service. Travelers who need language assistance or directions may get them by dialing the toll-free number.

The Travelodge employs 12 people, and during the busy summer season it adds four more. The Travelodge has made a practice in recent years of hiring the handicapped.

There are super-saver rates, senior citizens' discounts, a preferred traveler plan, government rates, a family plan, and the Sleepy Bear Club.

The Travelodge is active in the community, including working with the Boy Scouts and senior citizens. Jim Stiles believes that a healthy community is a better place for business to grow and flourish. Stiles owns 50 per-

Centrally located at 222 Grand Avenue in Waukegan, The Travelodge is convenient to shopping, the harbor marina, theaters, restaurants, and the city's Historic District.

cent of The Travelodge, and Forte Hotels International owns the other half.

The Travelodge is currently undergoing a major renovation—a new facade and redecoration of every room. The new exterior has been planned to blend in with new construction in Waukegan's downtown.

Chicago and Milwaukee are less than an hour's drive away. Each city offers major-league sports, music, art, and cultural, shopping, and eating experiences enough to satisfy almost any taste and budget. Great America, west of The Travelodge, is open from May through the first week of October. This large theme park offers rides, restaurants, and other activities.

The Waukegan harbor, marina, and beach is busy April through October with fishermen. Waukegan is known as the Freshwater Salmon Capital of the World. Visitors can enjoy a large array of sail- and power pleasure boats in the marina, as well as swimming, sunbathing, and ethnic festivals on the sandy beaches. All are within walking distance of The Travelodge.

The Travelodge in Waukegan, as do all Travelodges in North America, offers rooms that have been specially converted for its nonsmoking guests.

DEXTER PACKAGING AND SPECIALTY COATINGS

The Midland Division of Dexter Corporation was founded in Waukegan in 1939, primarily as a supplier of coatings to the U.S. government. Midland grew to become one of the largest diversified producers of specialty coatings for a variety of commercial, industrial, and consumer industries.

In 1963 Midland became part of Dexter Corporation, a *Fortune* 500 company producing specialty materials and the oldest company listed on the New York Stock Exchange. Dexter was founded in 1767. In 1988 The Dexter Corporation divided Midland into two separate divisions: Dexter Packaging Products and Dexter Specialty Coatings.

Dexter coatings are recognized worldwide for advanced research and development and technological capabilities that offer performance as well as economic advantages.

New 5,000-gallon polymer reactors in Hayward, California, and Birmingham, Alabama, complement the resin facilities in Waukegan, Illinois, to provide Dexter with the ability to develop and manufacture more complex types of polymers and resins, as well as proprietary formulations for a variety of market applications. Other plants are located in Deeside, Wales; Tournus, France; and Singapore. Joint ventures are located in Japan, Mexico, Canada, Venezuela, and Italy.

Dexter's traditional philosophy and emphasis on specialization is just as true today. Dexter's trained and ex-

Today the Dexter Packaging Products and Dexter Specialty Coatings divisions are international in scope, and both have headquarters in this lakeside facility in Waukegan, Illinois.

perienced staff, many of whom hold advanced degrees in the sciences, work closely with customers in the United States and overseas to identify problems, implement solutions, and apply Dexter technology.

The company offers research and development and technical service support to all its customers. This added value commitment is the key to Dexter's success and reputation for excellence as an innovator and leader in coatings and polymer technology.

The Packaging Products Division's four main lines include coatings for beverage cans, food cans, closures, and general packaging. Much of this group's emphasis in recent years has focused on the conversion from solventborne to waterborne products. Dexter has invested heavily in efforts to refine its waterborne technology and is the first coatings supplier to offer a waterborne system for drawn food cans.

Research and development efforts have also led to the development of a unique vinyl resin technology that offers superior performance on steel and aluminum beverage cans.

In the food segment, Dexter Packaging has a leading technology for the coating of two-piece drawn-redrawn cans, an area that is expected to see significant growth in the coming years.

The Specialty Coatings Division is recognized for its specially formulated products developed for the recreational and sporting goods, metal office furniture, military, automotive, aerospace, and cookware and bakeware markets. The group has aggressively pursued the development of a variety of customized and proprietary formulas that use lower polluting, lower energy cure technologies, including waterborne, high solids, solid powders, ultraviolet curing mechanisms, and two package systems.

Dexter Bouvet, France, has pioneered excellent coating products that have made the company the European leader in finishes for the wood industry.

The Specialty Coatings Division also provides a broad-based coil coating product line designed for the coil coating of metal stock used in prefabricated buildings, architectural components, and construction markets. With advanced capabilities in the areas of silicone polyester, polyester, and epoxy technologies, The Dexter Corporation anticipates heading the market for years to come.

Founded as the Midland Industrial Finishes Co. in 1939, the firm then primarily supplied coatings to the U.S. government.

NOSCO INC.

NOSCO Inc. is recognized by pharmaceutical and commercial companies throughout the United States as one of the country's foremost printing specialists of customized folding cartons, promotional literature, inserts/outserts, labels, and general advertising.

Founded in 1906, NOSCO has developed into a full-service printing company encompassing both skilled craft personnel and state-of-the-art technology in the areas of composing, litho preparation, press equipment, carton die cutting and gluing, folding, bindery, and other specialized services.

NOSCO's beginning can be traced to the founding of Zion, Illinois, in 1901 by the religious visionary, John Alexander Dowie. Dowie recognized that jobs created by flourishing businesses and industries were an essential aspect of support for the local population.

Among the businesses of the day was the Zion Printing and Publishing House. In 1906, six local businessmen purchased the office supply inventory of the publishing house and established the Zion Office Supply Company. As the firm gained national attention and scope, the name was changed to the National Office Supply Company (NOSCO).

As the office supply market expanded, a need for business cards, letterheads, and other printed items was soon discerned. This led to the addition

One-color offset printing—late 1930s.

of printing capability and the purchase of two small presses.

In 1913 George W. Morris joined NOSCO. He later became one of the majority stockholders, and in 1925 moved the firm to its present location in Waukegan.

NOSCO's growth was aided by the nearby location of Abbott Laboratories in North Chicago. In the early 1930s Abbott's business was beginning to flourish, and the drug company had a significant need for pharmaceutical printed products. Thus was born a strong business relationship between the two firms.

During the next 40 years the printing and folding carton manufacturing capability of NOSCO grew as the needs of Abbott Laboratories and other pharmaceutical companies expanded. In 1977 NOSCO's office supply business was sold to BAT, Inc., a local Zion, Illinois, firm in a related field. NOSCO

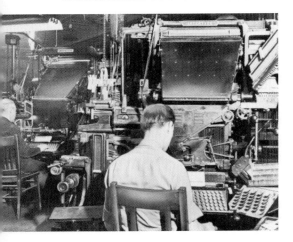

Setting type pre-World War II.

was retained as the official company name.

NOSCO was sold in September 1980 to Mercantile Holdings, Inc., a subsidiary of CRL, Inc., which is a privately controlled Delaware corporation.

All jobs are custom ordered and produced to customer specifications. The sales mix is folding cartons, 43 percent, and general advertising, 20 percent. NOSCO's specialization in pharmaceutical printing means that it is fully able to meet the stringent quality controls needed for full compliance with customer demands. Pharmaceutical customers account for 60 percent of NOSCO's sales.

In 1980, the year NOSCO was purchased by Mercantile Holdings, Inc., sales were slightly more than $8 million. By fiscal 1988 sales had surpassed $18 million. The majority of sales are generated locally in the greater Chicago area, although products are shipped worldwide.

NOSCO has nine full-time sales personnel and a contractual arrangement with Cannon Graphics, a New Jersey firm that sells folding cartons on

NOSCO's behalf to several East Coast pharmaceutical companies.

The Abbott account has three full-time NOSCO employees as account representatives. Among other major NOSCO customers are such well-known firms as Bantam Books, K mart, Kemper Group, Lyphomed, Kraft, Inc., Parker Pen, Searle Pharmaceuticals, Ray-o-vac, Jockey International, Snap-On Tools, Sterling Drugs, Alberto Culver, Baxter, Inc., and Walgreen Laboratories.

All functions, ranging from typesetting, camera, stripping, printing, die cutting, folding, gluing, and bindery services, are available in house. With more than a dozen specialized presses, NOSCO has an unequaled flexibility to produce outstanding printing, both in quantity and quality. NOSCO can

Two-color letterpress—1950s.

also offer unusually fast delivery time—three to four weeks from design to delivery can be achieved.

The company has kept pace with printing technology and automation, and has in-house computerized typesetting equipment, prepress equipment, the finest in cameras, automatic film processing, step and repeat machinery, and complete platemaking

facilities.

The flagships of NOSCO's wide range of services are its six-color offset presses. These high-speed, quick make-ready machines are designed to handle small or large runs on light paper up to and including folding carton board. These presses have the precision to give absolutely perfect registration and uniformity throughout the run.

NOSCO has the flexibility to provide carton containers for elegant perfume vials to complex hard-sell floor or counter displays. Special shapes, windows, and cold embossing are but a few of the innovations NOSCO has the capability of producing.

Rigid quality-control procedures and strict security measures from incoming raw material to the finished product and final delivery are under constant surveillance.

The only services NOSCO routinely purchases outside are color separations and lasar dies. Several quality trade shops are nearby and provide excellent quality, service, and pricing.

The NOSCO physical facility is a 100,000-square-foot manufacturing and administration building that has expanded from the original 20,000-square-foot structure that was built in 1925. In 1987 an additional 26,000-

square-foot building was purchased for warehousing and specialized manufacturing services.

NOSCO employs a staff of more than 200, with additional part-time workers to meet production requirements. Employee turnover at the firm traditionally has been low. Not only can several generations of one family be found working for NOSCO, it is not unusual to find people with more than

NOSCO's newest six-color offset press represents the latest in printing press technology.

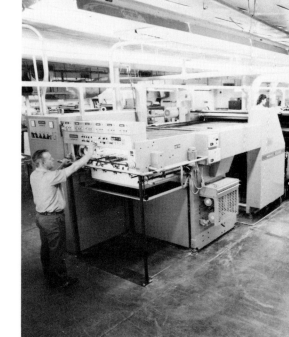

40 years' service with the company.

NOSCO Inc. intends to continue to enhance its reputation in the pharmaceutical and health care industries where stringent quality and service demands are routinely expected. With the continuing expansion of state-of-the-art equipment and dedicated personnel, a strong emphasis is also being placed on achievement of a similar reputation for high-quality four-color process printing oriented toward advertising and consumer markets.

UNIVERSITY OF HEALTH SCIENCES/THE CHICAGO MEDICAL SCHOOL

The history of University of Health Sciences/The Chicago Medical School has become an integral part of American medical education. As a privately supported, independent institution, it has managed to maintain a position of excellence as a national and community resource for more than 77 years.

Founded in 1912, The Chicago Medical School is fully accredited by the Liaison Committee of Medical Education of the American Medical Association and the Association of American Medical Colleges; the University of Health Sciences itself is accredited by the North Central Association. They have been a part of Lake County since the fall of 1980, when the medical school opened the doors of its 92.3-acre campus on Green Bay Road in North Chicago.

In 1967 a new era in health professions education began with the formation of University of Health Sciences, which, with The Chicago Medical School, became one of the first schools in the country committed to developing interlocking education programs for both physicians and related health professions. The university encompasses a School of Related Health Sciences, a School of Graduate and Postdoctoral Studies, as well as the medical school. The School of Related Health Sciences awards baccalaureate and master's degrees in medical technology, physical therapy, and nursing (the latter in conjunction with Barat College in Lake Forest), thus providing a supply of badly needed, highly skilled allied health professionals. To encourage upward career advancement, opportunities are provided, when possible, for students to make use of their previous employment experiences and to continue working in the field. The school also offers many options for part-time students.

The School of Graduate and Postdoctoral Studies was established for graduate and postdoctoral training in biological and health-related sciences,

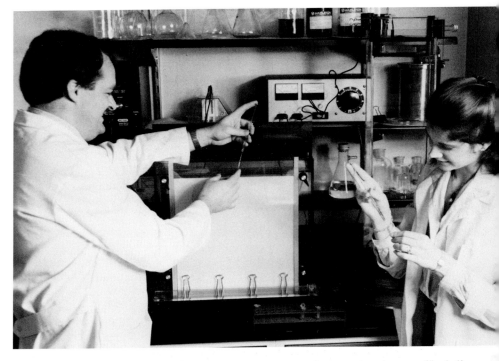

Dr. Kenneth Beaman (left), assistant professor, and Lea Baldini, a biotechnologist at UHS/CMS, work together in the analysis of genes—one of the many key research projects now under way at the North Chicago campus.

offering opportunities to earn advanced degrees (M.S. and/or Ph.D.) in anatomy, biochemistry, clinical psychology, medical physics, microbiology, pathology, pharmacology, and physiology. The School of Graduate and Postdoctoral Studies, together with The Chicago Medical School, offers combined M.D.-M.S. and M.D.-Ph.D. degree programs in most subjects. The school's major aim is to provide graduate-level education designed to meet the rapidly expanding need for highly qualified biomedical teachers and researchers in the health care field.

The $40-million, 350,000-square-foot Basic Science Building that opened in 1980 currently houses university and medical school administrative offices, the basic science departments, research and teaching laboratories, classrooms, auditoriums, dining facilities, a learning resource

center, and an extensive medical library. Other buildings are planned for what will eventually be a $100-million campus.

As part of its involvement in countywide health, UHS/CMS has developed meaningful affiliations with the North Chicago Veterans' Administration and Great Lakes Naval Training Center hospitals, in addition to maintaining important clinical and cooperative agreements with both Cook County and Mount Sinai hospitals in Chicago. Once established in Lake County, UHS/CMS was a founding force, together with Mayor Bobby Thompson of North Chicago and chief Ernest Fisher of the North Chicago Police Department, in the establishment of North Chicago Citizens Against Drug and Alcohol Abuse. UHS/CMS also opened its door to, and holds active membership in, numerous organizations that hold both meetings and special events on its campus—the Waukegan/Lake County Chamber of Commerce, the North Chicago Chamber of Commerce, the North Chicago Rotary, the Lake County Cancer Society, the Lake County Coalition Against Domestic Violence, and others.

In a program developed by CMS, medical students teach basic health classes on a voluntary basis to area schoolchildren, help raise foodstuffs and disposables for needy area families, and promote better exercise and conditioning through an annual 10K run. The UHS/CMS Computer Center is affiliated with both the College of Lake County and Lake Forest College in the development of a cooperative program in computer sciences.

The opening in 1982 of its Robert R. McCormick University Clinics provided county residents professional health care by highly qualified, experienced physicians. The clinical faculty of The Chicago Medical School are available to consult with patients and area physicians in all areas of medical

University of Health Sciences/The Chicago Medical School opened the doors of its 92.3-acre campus in North Chicago in 1980 with the commitment to make a major contribution toward solutions to health-related problems in Lake County and surrounding areas.

and surgical specialty. Among services available are prompt treatment of acute illnesses and injuries; diagnosis and treatment of patients through availability of a primary care Vascular Center, Podiatry Center, a Breast Care Center, a Dermatology Clinic, a Pediatric Center, and an ENT Clinic; in-house state-of-the-art technology such as Magnetic Resonance Imaging, a

General Electric CGR Mammographic, and Doppler Ultrasound equipment; and an industrial medicine program.

Added to the presence of all these available facilities is the easy access of the University Clinics. They are no more than 25 minutes from almost any Lake County location; free parking is available; flexible hours are designed to suit work schedules; and the clinics accept any type of traditional Illinois-based insurance coverage, including Champus.

The Chicago Medical School recognized many years ago that its obligation extended beyond the education of students to become competent, responsible, and concerned physicians. The school seeks to help all physicians to acquire postgraduate knowledge and skills through continuing medical education.

This is no small commitment to make since one of every 10 active physicians in the Chicago metropolitan area is a graduate of The Chicago Medical School. Graduates of The Chicago Medical School have gone on to distinguished private practice careers in every medical specialty, and many serve on the faculties of major medical schools where they pursue important research. Others participate in administrative capacities at hospitals and governmental agencies where they continue to improve the quality of medical care for millions of Americans. Of the more than 3,900 CMS alumni who are currently in active practice throughout the nation and the world, in excess of

1,000 practice in the State of Illinois, almost half of those in Chicagoland.

Each year between 10 and 15 symposia on a wide variety of medically related topics are sponsored by the Office of Continuing Medical Education. This program is fully accredited by the Accreditation Council for Continuing Medical Education.

UHS/CMS has produced a weekly radio series, "Chicago Medical School Reports," which has aired Sundays over local ABC-affiliate stations WXLC (102.3 FM) and WKRS (1220 AM). This unique public service program covers a broad variety of medical and health-related topics. In March 1989 it began its seventh consecutive year on the air.

In such a stimulating, multi-faceted environment, a remarkable and diverse blend of health disciplines is devoted exclusively to educating men and women for a broad range of professional careers in health care and research. This requires that students, faculty, administration, and the community work together to create an atmosphere that will lead toward a new era in establishing Lake County as one of the greatest health care centers of the United States.

The educational and research programs of University of Health Sciences/The Chicago Medical School are enhanced by the availability of a state-of-the-art learning resource center, including a large university library. Computers, high-tech equipment, audiovisuals, books, and more than 1,300 medical journals are all available for use by students and faculty.

HIGHLAND PARK HOSPITAL

Since its founding in 1918, Highland Park Hospital has been a community hospital with community support. It offers personal comfort and "high-touch" care, while moving toward more sophisticated and specialized service.

Highland Park Hospital offers programs not normally found in a community hospital. There are more than 350 physicians on the hospital's staff, and they specialize in more than 40 areas. The hospital's staff offers the highest level of care in a homelike environment, with advanced medical services usually only found in major urban medical centers.

The hospital offers a broad scope of cardiology services, including an adult dedicated cardiac catheterization laboratory. Cardiac catheterization is the most comprehensive diagnostic procedure available for the heart. The hospital also offers comprehensive diagnosis, treatment, and rehabilitation programs for cardiac patients.

A Cholesterol Control Program tries to help those patients with increased cholesterol levels in order to reduce their risk of heart attack. The program includes nutrition counseling.

Highland Park Hospital is a Level II Trauma Center, part of a statewide system of trauma centers that provides advanced care for those who are seriously injured. Patients brought to Highland Park Hospital are cared for by medical professionals specifically trained to treat serious trauma.

Laser surgery has thrust the hospital into the forefront with diverse laser capabilities across specialties. Surgical procedures in ophthalmology and gynecology, as well as pulmonary and breast laser surgeries that seemed impossible a few years ago, are routine today. Highland Park Hospital was one of the first in the entire Chicago area to remove pulmonary tumors using the YAG laser. The Eye Center provides the diagnostic and treatment capabilities usually found only at major teaching hospitals.

For cancer patients, the hospital's Oncology Unit is equipped and staffed to treat all types of cancer and related disorders on both an inpatient and outpatient basis. Treatments include surgery, chemotherapy, and outpatient radiation therapy.

The hospital's diabetes patient education program is one of the first nationwide to be recognized by the American Diabetes Association in accordance with the ADA's national standards. The needs of a maturing America are addressed by the hospital in the form of Mature Health®, a free membership program of comprehensive coordinated services appealing to all segments of the mature adult population and to those caregivers responsible for them. Mature Health has a membership of more than 4,000. The program provides a card containing vital information needed in case of an emergency, assistance with hospital billing and with Medicare and other in-

Two faces of Highland Park Hospital—the computer center of the hospital's Cardiac Catheterization Laboratory (below), and the warmth and tender loving care of a hospital volunteer (facing page).

surance problems, and help in meeting needs for items such as wheelchairs, warm meals, or transportation. It offers discounts on selected hospital services, information about health and wellness programs, and a quarterly newsletter.

There is also a program for older adults who need a structured social setting. The Alternative Adult Day Service offers the senior citizen a supervised social environment with planned activities and events. Participants can stay busy and enjoy themselves all day, and go home at night.

Two other examples of Highland Park Hospital's outreach are home health services and health education. Home health services respond to the needs of those unable to care independently for themselves at home. Nurses maintain a continuity of care between hospital and home; they ensure that patients receive the same quality of treatment at home. Community education programs produce a wide variety of educational opportunities for people in the communities served by the hospital. Highland Park Hospital provides health screenings and other services at many community events.

The Hoover Skilled Nursing Center serves patients who no longer require acute hospital care but can benefit from short-term skilled nursing and rehabilitative services. Patients convalesce under the watchful eyes of trained professionals, and acute care is close by if needed.

The hospital's Maternity Center offers the latest in labor and delivery, state-of-the-art equipment, and educational programs that invite the whole family to take part in the birthing process. A system of mother-baby care enables the same nurses to bring personalized care to both mother and baby.

Another example of personalized child care is the hospital's Loving Arms® program, made possible by the Neal Allen Winer Memorial Fund. A

program for sick children of up to 12 years of age, Loving Arms frees parents to go to work secure in the knowledge that their youngsters will be well cared for during the day. The hospital's trained pediatric nursing staff lovingly cares for the ill child.

Other health services include the treatment of eating disorders; inpatient and outpatient care for chemical dependency, including an outpatient adolescent program; and a full range of psychiatric services for inpatient and outpatient adults and adolescents.

Major contributors to the workings of the hospital are the Auxiliary and the Volunteers. Auxiliary members donate more than 70,000 hours per year for fund raising, service, and educational activities. Hospital volunteers perform some 40 vital services, assisting in patient care and with administrative tasks.

In 1982 Highland Park Hospital opened the Grove Medical Center in Long Grove to bring primary care to residents of the communities northwest of Highland Park. It is a comprehensive facility providing the services of more than 25 Highland Park Hospital physicians and medical specialists.

Highland Park Hospital also operates The Physician Finder®, a program that offers information about the physicians on the hospital medical staff and the hospital's many services. The Physician Finder can help a new resident, one replacing a doctor who has retired or relocated, one looking for a doctor convenient to home or work, and one seeking a doctor who accepts his or her insurance coverage.

Highland Park Hospital has an ongoing commitment to its community and to its patients to ensure the excellence of its medical services while keeping up with the changes in health care delivery. The hospital intends to continue to provide high-quality health care services that meet the needs of the people it serves with sensitivity and compassion.

AMERICAN NATIONAL BANK OF LIBERTYVILLE

American National Bank of Libertyville has the capacity of a large downtown bank and is the bank for business in Lake County. In addition to business banking, American National Bank is committed to community banking, providing its customers with personalized attention. The institution offers a wide range of services to accommodate all business and personal lending and depository needs for its customers. As the area has grown, the bank has grown with it, with assets of more than $200 million and $125 million in loans outstanding.

The bank was founded in 1892 when Libertyville was a farming community with a population of only 800. The closest bank was in Waukegan. Five prominent businessmen recognized the need for a bank in Libertyville, and each invested $1,000 to open the Lake County Bank on April 4, 1892, at 525 North Milwaukee Avenue. After the first day of business, deposits totaled $20,000.

In 1903, to counter competition from a national bank, the institution was reorganized under the name Lake County National Bank. In 1932 the two institutions merged to become First Lake County National Bank. The following year a moratorium was de-

Five prominent businessmen, seeing a need for a bank in Libertyville, invested $1,000 each and opened the Lake County Bank in 1892. The forerunner to American National Bank of Libertyville was at 525 North Milwaukee Avenue.

Today the American National Bank of Libertyville is located at 1201 South Milwaukee Avenue.

clared for all banks in the country. The bank, which had wide community support, resumed operations in July of that year with total capital of $65,000.

In 1942 the bookkeeping department consisted of two people doing the checking account posting on two high-back posting machines. Loans were made from teller windows. There were no applications or credit checks; the bank knew its small number of customers personally. A customer's word and signature were his bond and collateral. Services were limited to checking and savings accounts, loans, and safe deposit boxes.

At the end of World War II the bank began to grant mortgages. Interest rates were stable. Savings accounts paid 2.5 percent per year, and mortgage loans were 4.5 to 5 percent.

In the 1960s, due to a strong calling program, bank by mail, several innovative products, and a sales-oriented staff, the bank experienced strong growth necessitating the construction of the building at 140 West Cook Avenue.

As Libertyville grew to the south and business banking was flourishing, a new and thoroughly modern structure was built in 1979 and the bank moved to its present location, 1201 South Milwaukee Avenue, and re-

tained the 140 West Cook building as a facility. That same year the bank's holding company, First Lake County Corporation, was formed.

As the 1980s began it was clear that the community's growth required resources beyond the capacity of a local bank. Business customers especially were asking for sophisticated services and the higher lending capacity of a larger bank. Yet neither the shareholders nor the board of directors wanted to lose the bank's local decision-making ability and its community focus.

The directors looked for a suitable partner to merge with and found the right candidate in American National Bank of Chicago. The change in ownership was completed in August 1983, and the name of the bank was changed to American National Bank of Libertyville in January 1984. This change has been beneficial for the bank as well as for the community. The bank has a greater ability to serve the increasing number of businesses and new customers in the Libertyville market, and at the same time is well able to maintain its traditional close relationships with its present diverse base of loyal customers.

With the continued dedication of its talented staff, American National Bank of Libertyville will maintain its current high level of service and its contribution to the growth of Libertyville and surrounding communities.

NORTH SHORE GAS COMPANY

A North Shore Gas Company float in the Highland Park Day parade in the 1930s.

North Shore Gas Company, headquartered in Waukegan, provides gas service to more than 108,000 customers in 56 communities in a 275-square-mile area of northeastern Illinois. North Shore Gas owns and operates 1,740 miles of gas mains and a peak-shaving plant. It is a subsidiary of Chicago-based Peoples Energy Corporation and a sister company of The Peoples Gas Light & Coke Company, with which it shares many facilities and services.

North Shore Gas serves a growing area in Lake County, where the sustained housing boom shows no signs of abating. The growing numbers of shopping centers, office parks, hotels, and other business developments look to gas for its reliability, efficiency, and lower operating costs.

Through North Shore's aggressive purchasing of low-cost gas, as well as the company's careful supply management and introduction of technological improvements in operations and customer service, Lake County residents and businesses enjoy gas rates that are among the country's lowest. Customers now have the option of purchasing gas directly from producers or marketers, and engaging North Shore Gas to transport it to a customer's premises. In addition, improved technologies such as gas air conditioning and cogeneration are gaining the attention of more large Lake County customers.

To help meet the future energy needs of Lake County's growing population, North Shore Gas has built a large, modern regional operations center in Mundelein, at Route 60 and Butterfield Road. The three-building, 40,000-square-foot complex houses a variety of company operations, including distribution, service, transportation, and warehouse activities.

Another recent technological advance includes state-of-the-art, hand-held recording devices that permit faster and more accurate reading of customers' meters. And a new generation of equipment is being tested that allows the reading of meters from a moving vehicle.

North Shore Gas began in 1883, when the fledgling Waukegan Gas Company began its operations in a one-room gas plant, just 20 feet square. The firm turned on Waukegan street lamps and interior lights to illuminate, for the first time, the court house, opera building, and several downtown stores.

Waukegan and its neighboring North Shore communities grew quickly and, along with that growth, gas lamps began to appear in North Chicago, Lake Bluff, Lake Forest, Highwood, and Highland Park.

By the time the gaslight era flickered to a close early in this century, the North Shore Gas name was well established, and the company was developing new gas markets.

Originally the firm manufactured illuminating gas from a process using hard coal and crude oil. To produce a fuel for cooking and heating, North Shore switched to more advanced gas-making processes, using coke ovens that yielded gas from coal and water-gas units that made gas from coke by-products. In 1947 natural gas began moving via pipelines from producing fields in Texas to North Shore's markets. As this economical and clean form of pipeline gas grew to become the major source of North Shore's supply, the company began to phase out its gas manufacturing equipment.

North Shore Gas Company has been a pivotal force in the impressive development within Lake County and other portions of northeastern Illinois. And it intends to play an equally important role far into the future.

North Shore Gas Company's new regional operations center in Mundelein was completed in 1988.

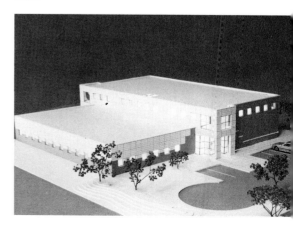

INTRUPA

Intrupa, headquartered in Grayslake, services the materials-handling industry with quality parts and fast, same-day service. Intrupa is first in the after-market parts field for domestic and foreign lift trucks and in-plant vehicles, with parts on hand for more than 45,000 different OEM applications.

Intrupa's commitment to quality and service goes beyond just parts, as demonstrated by dedicated and experienced personnel, continued product expansion, and a professional, customer-oriented dealer network.

Another aspect of Intrupa's business is the repair of electronic controls, which it has been doing for more than a decade. The firm's highly qualified repair technicians have years of training and experience. Only the finest repair components and newest equipment available are used. Where applicable, controls being serviced are updated to the latest available version.

The Intrupa story begins with its founder, Hans Anger, who came to the United States in 1957. He arrived in New York in February of that year from Germany with his wife and three small children. The family's American sponsor, however, had died. Promised employment for Anger had vanished. Anger, fluent in Spanish, German, and English, talked to many people about job prospects, and he was frequently urged to go to Chicago, a city of opportunity.

The family arrived in Chicago on a Sunday. The next day Anger applied for a job in the export department of a company selling forklift parts. He was hired that day.

After two years with the firm, he decided to strike out on his own. Even though he held two jobs, one with the Victor Adding Machine Company and the other as a moonlighting clerk at Sears, Roebuck and Co., he began what was to become Intrupa in the family's third-floor Chicago apartment at 5201 North Magnolia.

Anger started making electrical

From left: Peter Anger, Hans Anger, Jr., Hans Anger, Sr., and Andy Anger.

contacts on the kitchen stove. He would buy the copper bars and silver alloy, and braze them with a hand-held propane torch. The Anger youngsters would help in the assembly, cleaning, and packaging. In 1960 Intrupa, which stands for Industrial Truck Parts, was officially incorporated. The children were eight, six, four, and two years old.

Initially, orders for the electrical contacts came from the federal government for battery-powered forklift trucks. Intrupa was still a one-man, one-family show. Soon Anger was selling his contacts to lift truck dealers for replacement parts.

By 1962 Anger was working full time in his business. Days of 16 to 18

hours were not uncommon. His children would help make the contacts, package them, and see to it that they were ready to be sold. Anger then would drive around the midwestern states in his camper to meet customers and potential customers. Sales increased and the firm grew at a steady pace.

Also in 1962 the company moved to its first official headquarters, at 5145 North Clark Street in Chicago. The firm continued making contacts, but was also wholesaling other products for lift trucks. Anger designed a turntable furnace that helped both automate and speed up production.

The firm grew at a steady pace and gradually expanded into the buildings next door on Clark Street.

There are good reasons for Intrupa's successful growth. One is that Hans Anger offered quality products at a lower price. He offered then, as he does today, same-day shipment of orders from stock. A second reason is that battery-powered lift trucks took over the market, as opposed to trucks powered by internal combustion engines. By 1980, 50 percent of the lift trucks were battery powered. As the industry grew, so did Intrupa.

In the early 1970s Intrupa decided to become a manufacturer in a bigger way. Initially this was accomplished by subcontracting machine work to make such parts as axles, shafts, and gears. The next step was to develop its own manufacturing plant. Anger bought into and then expanded a small, two-man manufacturing plant. Today the manufacturing shop runs three shifts, six days per week and employs nearly 50 people.

By 1970 Intrupa had outgrown the Clark Street location and moved to 4853 Ravenswood. From that time until its relocation to Grayslake in 1985,

Intrupa Manufacturing Company, Inc., Grayslake, Illinois, 1985.

The Ravenswood Building of Intrupa Manufacturing Company in 1970.

the firm expanded at its Ravenswood location until it had to rent a large warehouse nearby, and then later on Pulaski Avenue. The Ravenswood building was donated to the Chicago Historical Society in 1985.

Another important milestone in the company's development occurred in 1978 with the introduction of electronic circuit and control manufacturing. This activity takes place principally in Indiana, where there are 20 employees doing assembly and repair work. There is also a repair center in Grayslake.

It soon became apparent that the building on Ravenswood was too small for Intrupa's expanding operations. A decision to move was made, largely by Hans Anger's sons, who were active in the company and interested in pursuing the expansion of the firm. Grayslake was selected because Intrupa found an existing building of the right size and also because of its proximity to its manufacturing facility, which had been moved to Round Lake Beach four years earlier.

Industrial Revenue bonds were used to help acquire the new building, and Intrupa was aided in this effort by Grayslake National Bank.

While the space in the new building is 2.5 times greater than that in Chicago, Intrupa is once again fully utilizing all the space it has. The firm is again thinking of expanding.

Today the company is managed by Hans Jr., who was named president early in 1988. Hans Anger, Sr., 62, is currently recovering from a severe stroke. The entire company is looking forward to the day when he is able to return to his post as chairman. Intrupa is the largest supplier of aftermarket parts to the lift truck industry. The firm has four locations: Grayslake; Round Lake Beach; Walkerton, Indiana; and Toronto, Canada.

Intrupa operates under the philosophy formulated by its founder. Free catered lunches have always been provided for employees. There is double pay for vacations, profit sharing, pension, and complete hospitalization and medical insurance. The company makes its Wisconsin vacation cottage available for employees' use, and the Anger family tries to maintain a happy environment by sponsoring numerous group outings, parties, and picnics.

Regarding the future, Intrupa is constantly expanding its product line and searching other markets for diversification.

GOOD SHEPHERD HOSPITAL

Good Shepherd Hospital, a 162-bed full-service health care facility located on Highway 22, two miles west of Route 59 near Barrington, serves residents of northwest Cook, southwest Lake, northeast Kane, and southeast McHenry counties. Good Shepherd is one of five hospitals that make up Evangelical Health Systems, the largest health care system in metropolitan Chicago.

At Good Shepherd, wholistic care is practiced in which one's emotional and spiritual as well as physical needs are addressed. A full range of inpatient and outpatient services, including day surgery, are offered. The emergency room is open 24 hours per day and is staffed by physicians who are trained specialists in emergency medicine, along with certified mobile intensive care telemetry nurses. The emergency medicine department also provides a poison control hotline.

On the staff are more than 240 physicians representing 35 medical specialties, an all-registered nurse staff that provides primary one-on-one care, and a team of allied health care professionals. Many of Good Shepherd's physicians practice on-site at the hospi-

Good Shepherd Hospital, a 162-bed health care facility located north of Barrington on Highway 22, is one of five hospitals that make up Evangelical Health Systems, the largest health care system in metropolitan Chicago.

The ground-breaking ceremony for Good Shepherd took place September 26, 1976, and literally was a community effort with hundreds of area residents pulling a plow over a portion of the future hospital site. The facility opened three years later on October 17, 1979.

tal's three doctors' office buildings.

Good Shepherd is state licensed to provide Level II intermediate care for newborns and continues to offer the state's largest hospital-based Lamaze program, prenatal nutrition and fitness sessions, a postnatal exercise class, and a caring kids course to prepare brothers- and sisters-to-be for the new baby. The department recently was remodeled to include single-room maternity suites along with previously offered options such as traditional delivery or use of a birthing chair.

A comprehensive mental health program was established in 1987 that includes a three-level integrated program of treatment and services for adults and adolescents. A closed 16-bed inpatient unit is located on the hospital's first floor to treat acute mentally ill patients. An addition has been constructed on the west end of the building for day hospital and specialty outpatient mental health services, including an adult alcohol substance abuse program.

Wellspring, Good Shepherd's women's health center, also opened in 1987. The center, located in the hospital, offers a women's health library, wellness education programs, a women's health resource line, and a specialized physician referral service. A second Wellspring center is available in Palatine.

Professional Home Health Care, Inc., is also a part of the Good Shepherd concept of wholistic medicine. This service offers quality health care in the convenience, comfort, and privacy of a patient's own home.

Good Shepherd provides a wide range of community education programs and services, including a Back School, Breathing Club, nutritional counseling and a Seniorcise class for persons age 60 and over. Mammography, hypertension, and osteoporosis risk screening programs are also available.

Good Shepherd's Auxiliary provides Telecare, a community outreach program for handicapped and elderly persons living alone, and A-HELP, a hospital equipment lending program. In addition, the hospital offers Lifeline, an emergency response system for individuals needing special medical assistance.

For business and industry as wel

as the community, Good Shepherd has HELP (Health Evaluation Lifestyle Programs). HELP includes a full range of health care services and wellness programs: preplacement and executive physicals, CPR training, a stop smoking clinic, a worker injury program, a diabetic management program, breast cancer detection classes, an Optifast program (to help severely obese patients lose weight through a protein-sparing modified fast), stress management classes, fitness screening, and Trim Team (a weight reduction program based on behavior modification principles).

Every Wednesday from 11:30 a.m.

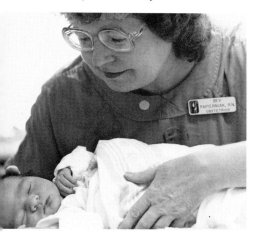

Good Shepherd Hospital is state licensed to provide Level II intermediate care for newborns and also offers the state's largest hospital based Lamaze program. The obstetrics department has comfortable single-room maternity suites that allow mothers to remain in one location throughout the labor, delivery, recovery, and postpartum periods.

to noon, listeners can tune in Good Shepherd's "Community Health Update" radio show on WAIT-AM 850. Featured on each program are physicians from Good Shepherd's medical staff and hospital health professionals who address high-interest health topics. The weekly shows are broadcast live so listeners can call during the programs and ask questions about the

health issues being discussed.

All of Good Shepherd's activities have the enthusiastic support of its Auxiliary and volunteer services. The Auxiliary of Good Shepherd, easily one of the strongest and most dedicated in the country, is made up of 1,100 men, women, and teens who provide about 80,000 hours of service each year.

Pledges and gifts of more than one million dollars are made possible through a variety of fund-raising events sponsored by Auxiliary members: Catchpenny, the resale and craft shop in downtown Barrington; the Pear Tree Gift Shop in the ground-floor lobby of the hospital; the Pear Tree Cafe & Cupboard, which serves a variety of sandwiches and salads; the Art in the Barn exhibition held every September; and the Luv-Ewes group, which makes handcrafted items sold at Catchpenny.

Adult volunteers and volunteens work in 30 different departments as receptionists, typists, patient escorts, clerks, messengers, as well as in other positions that make a hospital function smoothly. A patient recreation group meets weekly to assemble kits for patients and make tray favors and special gifts for the pediatrics unit and nursery.

Long before Good Shepherd's opening in 1979, the Auxiliary worked to bring a hospital to the area. The Cary Grove chapter of the Auxiliary for a Proposed Area Hospital was formed in 1966, followed by Barrington, Lake Zurich-Long Grove, and Wauconda-Island Lake chapters. Three years later a Joint Committee for an Area Hospital made up of representatives from 15 area communities was developed to pursue the goal.

The Evangelical Hospital Association—now Evangelical Health Systems—became the agency through which these efforts were drawn together. In 1970 the association agreed to undertake the development of the hospital and allocated funds to study its

Comprehensive 24-hour emergency care is provided at Good Shepherd. The state has designated the hospital as a Level II Trauma Center.

feasibility. Quaker Oats provided the 300-acre site by gift and purchase. The Illinois Health Facilities Planning Board approved the building of Good Shepherd in 1976, and construction began in the fall of that year.

Good Shepherd's parent organization, Evangelical Health Systems (EHS), was founded in 1906 and is related to the United Church of Christ.

The corporation's operations include four other hospitals (Christ Hospital and Medical Center, Oak Lawn; Good Samaritan Hospital, Downers Grove; South Chicago Community Hospital, Chicago; and Bethany, Chicago), outpatient services, home health care, extended care facilities, retirement complexes, physicians' office buildings, a counseling network for individuals and families, and a wholistic health center.

In keeping with EHS' United Church of Christ heritage, the system's 9,000 employees, more than 1,500 affiliated physicians, plus auxilians and volunteers maintain a Christian emphasis in all their endeavors.

UARCO INCORPORATED
BUSINESS FORMS

For nearly a century UARCO has provided communications products and services for business ranging from the largest to the smallest, but its years of experience in the design of systems and forms, in forms management, in cost-efficient production, and in its reliability as a supplier make UARCO a particularly valuable partner for the larger corporation.

The process of business communication ranges from the handwritten record of a simple business transaction to sophisticated bar-coding systems. Business communications involves forms: forms for billing, collecting, controlling, receiving, shipping, marking, mailing, and promotion. Whatever the communication need, a form is required to control it.

A customer shopping at a small retail store will very likely receive a written receipt prepared on an autographic register, an UARCO innovation nearing a century of practical, everyday use in thousands of small businesses worldwide.

But when size and technology are added, the business communication problem then is a matter of controlling

The UARCO headquarters was built in 1962 slightly west of downtown Barrington, Illinois. Today more than 200 people work in these offices, and nearly 4,700 people are employed by the company nationwide.

thousands of orders for thousands of products, and the parts and raw materials needed to produce them in a large organization.

Over the years UARCO has built one of the most modern and geographically widespread production operations in the business forms industry. No matter where customers are, UARCO is nearby with 249 sales offices, 17 plants, and 24 distribution centers nationwide. Supporting UARCO's production facilities is an experienced engineering and research operation that tests and evaluates the papers, adhesives, inks, and carbons used to produce UARCO products.

Throughout its history, when equipment has not been available, UARCO has gone ahead and invented its own. Such experience helped the firm produce such new products as Data-Mailer (a self-mailer form),

TRIM-EDGE, E-Z-Read (green bar), Convelope (continuous envelope and special pocket forms), and Data Pocket.

UARCO offers a wide line of afterhandling equipment, including bursters, deleavers, imprinters, and shredders, all designed by UARCO to handle various form constructions and sizes.

UARCO has been a leader in the development of uses for bar coding and other optical scanning technologies, pressure-sensitive labeling, word-processing products, ink-jet imaging, forms-handling equipment, and forms management.

The company has developed forms systems for a wide range of vertical markets. These include health care, manufacturing, distribution, financial and governmental systems, and pharmaceutical and medical applications.

UARCO is also well known in the business forms industry for its outstanding and rigorous training programs for its sales representatives, who are carefully and extensively trained in design, products, technical information, and other topics. They are well schooled in the company's capabilities, and that enables them to get the job done right. There are more than 775 UARCO sales representatives nationwide, who are able to custom-design forms to precise specifications.

UARCO's forms management program is capable of handling all of a company's forms requirements. The firm can offer a plan to improve, control, and administer a client's total forms program.

With its Pick and Pack plan, UARCO will act as a company's supply room, print shop, forms vendor, and warehouse. This program provides an organization with forms and supplies on an as-needed basis.

UARCO's history began in the late 1800s, when a lawyer lost a case because he could not prove that his client, a storekeeper, had sold certain merchandise to a customer. There was no valid proof of sale.

The attorney decided that what businessmen needed was some way to make exact copies of transactions at the time of sale, copies that could not be altered without detection and would be accepted as evidence in a court of law. From this need, the first autographic register was developed, and the business forms industry was launched.

UARCO entered the scene in 1894, when a young Canadian machinist, England J. Barker, founded the United Autographic Register Company in Chicago. The firm grew rapidly, first manufacturing registers and handwritten forms. Then came forms for typewriters and other early business machines. The company flourished.

By 1922 the business had grown to such an extent that a plant was built in Oakland, California, to make UARCO products more readily available to companies on the West Coast. The plant soon outgrew its facility, and in 1936 a larger factory was acquired at Emeryville.

In 1928 the Mani-Fold Company of Cleveland, Ohio, was purchased, and

the following year still another firm was acquired, the Globe Register Company of Cincinnati. In 1930 a new plant was built in Chicago to house the former Globe Register Company. Despite the Depression, the plant prospered during the 1930s.

During World War II a large part of UARCO's facilities was devoted to the production of specialized forms for the government, war agencies, and businesses engaged in war work. As no essential changes in products or processes were necessary, UARCO was able to return to its commercial production with little interruption at the end of the war.

After the war UARCO concentrated on expanding production with new plants in Deep River, Connecticut, and Watseka, Illinois. During this period new forms were developed, including

State-of-the-art technology in each UARCO plant turns blank paper into printed forms and makes the company a reliable source of supply for thousands of customers.

ing continuous forms for typewriters, billing machines, and other office equipment.

A new headquarters was constructed in Barrington, Illinois, in 1962. New plants continued to be added as the company increased its products, staff, and list of customers. During the 1960s and 1970s plants were opened in Riverside, California; Adrian, Michigan; Roseburg, Oregon; Toccoa, Georgia; and Radcliff, Kentucky.

A direct-mail facility was set up in DeKalb, Illinois, during 1979 and 1980. Drummond Business Forms in Quebec, Canada, was acquired in 1970, and York Tape and Label in York, Pennsylvania, in 1982. Plant growth spread to Kennett, Missouri; Corning, Iowa; Fulton, Kentucky; Eupora, Mississippi; and Eudora, Kansas.

While much has changed since the early days, the objective of UARCO is still to produce a superior line of products to meet customer needs at fair prices.

WALGREENS

Walgreens is literally growing across America. Sales for 1988 reached well over $4 billion, produced primarily by 1,416 drugstores located in 650 communities in 29 states and Puerto Rico. Forty percent of those stores are new or acquired in the past three years, reflecting the company's commitment to planned growth.

In 1987 alone Walgreens opened 103 new drugstores, and during the past three years the company completed major remodelings, in excess of $100,000 each, on 269 stores, including the Medi Mart stores that were acquired in 1986. These remodeled stores are now more appealing, more contemporary in appearance, and more competitive. In 1988 Walgreens opened 88 new drugstores and remodeled 60 others. And Walgreens plans to average about 100 store openings annually over the next five years, excluding possible acquisitions.

Many of these new stores will be built in existing major markets, including the Chicago area, where 10 years ago there were 124 Walgreens. Today there are 239, with 20 new ones planned for the next two years.

When Walgreens' Belvidere Mall store opened, shoppers lined up for savings in every department.

Workmen install the sign outside Walgreens' soon-to-be-opened store in the Belvidere Mall in Waukegan in 1965. Today Walgreens operates two stores in the city—one in the Belvidere Mall and the other at 1401 Lewis Avenue.

This growth is possible for two reasons: the availability of "fill-in" spots in dynamic city neighborhoods, and a booming population in the suburbs, where developers are pouring millions of dollars into residential and shopping center construction. Lake County is certainly no exception to this activity.

The experience of the Chicago region holds true for established Walgreens markets such as Cincinnati, El Paso, Louisville, Memphis, Milwaukee, Minneapolis, New Orleans, St. Louis, and San Francisco.

The growth story is even stronger in Florida, where the population swells by 893 residents per day. Five of Walgreens' top 25 markets are located in that state, and as many as 50 locations are under consideration for new stores. Arizona is another high-growth state with 15 new locations approved in the Phoenix and Tucson markets over the next two years. More than half of all Walgreens drugstores nationwide have opened since 1982.

Walgreens operates the strongest prescription business in America, filling nearly 5 percent of all retail prescriptions, while operating 2.5 percent of all drugstores.

At Walgreens, the pharmacy is the core department that differentiates Walgreens from other retailers and adds a distinctly proprietary value to the business.

Intercom, Walgreens' on-line pharmacy computer system, is an invaluable marketing tool, offering the consumer prescription transferability, tax/insurance records, and 24-hour access to records in an emergency. With Intercom, Walgreens has defined a new kind of pharmacy service.

Walgreens believes in its basic business. As a nationwide drugstore chain, Walgreens is confident of its ability to grow and remain a profitable and respected force in retailing well into the twenty-first century. There is a sound basis for Walgreens' future expectations: 14 years of record sales and earnings. While its competitors diversified in the late 1970s and 1980s, Walgreens consolidated, disposing of businesses that did not fit its disciplined strategies and concentrating its energies on improving drugstore performance.

Several trends spell growth for Walgreens. In a period of skyrocketing health care costs, prescriptions are a bargain. Spending for pharmaceutical products in 1986 was less than 7 percent of the nation's total medical bill, down from 12 percent in the 1960s. The flow of new drug therapies anticipated through this century can only increase the positive impact of pharmaceuticals on the nation's health bill.

Another trend is the birth rate. New mothers are excellent drugstore customers, and children under two are high users of prescriptions and traditional drugstore items.

And consider Americans' shrinking leisure time. The average American had only 2.5 free hours per day in 1985, down from 3.75 hours in 1973. Dual-income couples with children have the least leisure time of all.

Convenient shopping is a powerful leverage for these time-pressed consumers. This trend bodes well for Walgreen-type stores—convenient, compact, fast-service outlets with an established health care identity. Walgreens is first and foremost a drugstore. The company continually refines its merchandise mix in favor of stronger health care coverage.

To increase shopping frequency

Walgreens Intercom pharmacy computer system is a "silent partner" in preparing prescriptions. By saving time and eliminating many routine tasks, Intercom can enable pharmacists to spend more time answering questions and explaining drugs. Intercom also provides special services, such as tax/insurance records and around-the-clock emergency medical information.

and support its convenience image, Walgreens has opened food centers in 500 stores, stocking dairy products, frozen foods, and hundreds of grocery staples. The goal is to satisfy customers' midweek food needs at prices competitive with major grocery chains. About half the company's new and remodeled stores now include food centers.

Since 40 percent of drugstore purchases are unplanned, drawing new customers and decreasing the time between shopping trips are Walgreen goals. Photofinishing has been part of this strategy since the 1920s and is

a high-growth segment of Walgreen business.

To support rapid growth, Walgreens has added 560,000 square feet of distribution space during the past several years, a 32-percent increase. Computer-supported management systems, electronic freight sortation, and computer-assisted order-selection devices are extensively used throughout the distribution network. Another major concern for the future is finding and retaining good employees. A career at Walgreens offers the advantages of success and growth.

The firm was founded in Chicago in 1901 by Charles R. Walgreen. In the 1920s a Walgreen employee invented the milkshake, and the company opened its first Waukegan drugstore.

Today Walgreens operates stores in the Belvidere Mall and at 1401 Lewis Avenue, and Charles R. Walgreen III, grandson of the company's founder, is Walgreens' chairman and chief executive.

UNIVERSAL OUTDOOR ADVERTISING

Universal Outdoor Advertising was founded in a kitchen in 1973 by William "Wild Bill" Smith, his son William "Marty" Smith III, and Dan Simon. Today it owns 200 billboards in Lake County, with 95 percent of them leased by local businesses. The firm offers complete outdoor advertising—from eight-sheet billboards to expressway bulletins.

Universal is headquartered in elegant new offices in the recently completed Quaker Tower just north of Chicago's Loop.

Universal has a wide range of billboards available to service the outdoor exposure needs of local businesses in Lake County. The billboards are placed near some of the most heavily traveled roads in the county. Billboards range in size from 6 feet by 12 feet (an eight-sheet in industry parlance) all the way up to 20 feet by 60 feet.

Businesses utilize billboard space in the sure knowledge that their highly visible message lets potential customers know of the ready availability and exact location of a product or service. Universal believes that billboards are a superior medium for advertising.

With radio and television, a message is only on the air for 30 seconds; a billboard message is up for all to see for 30 days to a year. A business can target its market area, have high visibility, and develop name recognition.

Universal has an extensive range of clients using its billboard space. Among them are builders, radio stations, newspapers, restaurants, auto dealers, and even pawn shops. Lakehurst Mall and Outboard Marine Corp. are two recent additions to the firm's client roster. Universal also buys billboards statewide for the Illinois State Lottery.

Universal offers full service to its customers. It will do the creative work needed to develop the copy and art that will help the billboard sell, and suggest sites that will maximize the value of a customer's billboard purchase.

The firm frequently hires men and women with a depth of experience in the field of billboard advertising. The company has trained crews who put up

Eye-catching outdoor displays by Universal.

the paper on the billboards, and it employs experienced painters for billboards that require painted artwork.

Universal believes in solving problems aggressively. It is flexible in its ability to give its customers what they want, and its management believes that the firm gives more in time, effort, and service than do other billboard companies.

In 1984 Universal developed its widely acclaimed campaign "Lake County—A Great Place to Live." The firm actively supports such efforts as

the annual Christmas Toys for Tots campaign, United Way, the Waukegan Symphony Orchestra, and the Northern Illinois Council on Alcohol and Substance Abuse. Marty Smith, Universal's president, has served as both a board member and as a director.

Vice-president Dan Simon has served as president of the Chicagoland Outdoor Association as well as president of the Independent Advertising Council, the Washington-based trade group that represents small to medium-size outdoor billboard operators. He also serves on the Small Business Administration's advisory council.

Universal Outdoor Advertising plans to expand by offering its services to more customers through selected acquisitions and entrance into new markets.

MEIER'S MASTERBILT MANUFACTURING HOME LEISURE CENTERS

Meier's Masterbilt Manufacturing Home Leisure Centers are located in Fox Lake and Bloomingdale. The company builds custom fences and pools, as well as sells casual furniture for a family's leisure and recreational activities.

Meier's Masterbilt carries a full line of items for home recreation, including pool tables and accessories, spas, saunas, woodburning stoves and fireplaces, whirlpool-jetted bathtubs, exercise equipment, game tables, boat piers, and a complete line of patio and outdoor furniture, as well as glassware

Meier's Masterbilt Manufacturing Home Leisure Centers just completed a 6,000-foot addition to its showroom in Fox Lake (above), as well as a brand new pool park (left), one of the largest such parks in the United States.

and place settings. Meier's sells a full complement of pool chemicals and other items that can be used to make indoor or outdoor swimming safe and enjoyable.

Currently Meier's has 25 crews supplying construction and service to its customers. All installations are done with Meier's own people, equipment, and materials. The company's commitment to service includes careful sales and product training for both store salespersons and for the installation crews. The firm services everything that it builds. To enhance its service capability, Meier's recently purchased a pool service van, which literally is a parts department on wheels.

Meier's likes to thank its longtime, loyal customers by inviting them to frequent closed-door sales. Meier's also

offers pool seminars. One seminar deals with pool opening, another with pool closing, and a third with pool maintenance. These information sessions are very popular with customers.

Founded in 1962, Meier's Masterbilt Manufacturing Company, Inc., has been building custom fences and pools since its inception. The company is led by Richard Scott, chairman and chief executive officer; Stephen Scott, president; Stephen Meier, executive vice-president; and Ron Davies, vice-president and chief financial officer. Frank Meier, founder and pool division manager, oversees all internal sales production and service within the pool division. Frank Meier's other sons, Michael and Kerry, are active in the firm, as are daughters Cindy and Lorrie.

As his business improved Meier saw the cost advantages of producing his own product, and he soon built a fence manufacturing plant. Meier's still sells chain-link fences, as well as wrought-iron and ornamental aluminum fencing.

Above-ground swimming pools were added, and then in-ground pools.

Because the installation of fences and pools is highly seasonal, Meier looked for a way to keep his business flourishing 12 months per year and to provide his employees with year-round work. He introduced pool tables and then casual furniture.

Today Meier's has more than 30,000 items in stock, and the firm in 1986 completed the construction of a 20,000-square-foot vaulted warehouse. The inventory is completely computer controlled, making it easier to keep accurate track of pickups and deliveries and to service customer inquiries.

In 1984 Meier's opened its second store in west suburban Bloomingdale, where it is the anchor tenant in the Circle Center Mall. Bloomingdale was chosen because it is an area of growth.

Meier's has just completed a 6,000-foot addition to its showroom in Fox Lake, as well as a brand-new pool park just outside the showroom. The park, with four in-ground pools and eight above-ground pools, is one of the largest such parks in the United States.

Meier's believes in marketing aggressively. The firm uses newspaper advertising, direct mail, and the *Yellow Pages.* Other important sources of new business include referrals from satisfied customers.

Meier's plans to open several new stores in the next few years in the Chicagoland area.

THE FIRST NATIONAL BANK OF WAUKEGAN

The story of The First National Bank of Waukegan begins in 1852. Only a few years before, in 1849, the town of Little Fort had become the village of Waukegan with a population of 3,500. Its story is a history of banking in Lake County. The bank in its early years was the sole bank between Chicago and Kenosha.

In 1852 money was scarce, and the value of what there was could not be trusted; the panic lay only a few years ahead. It was also in that year that Charles and Ransom Steele founded the private banking firm of C.R. and R. Steele, Bankers, the institutional ancestor of today's The First National Bank.

Waukegan became an important link with the region's farmers upon the completion of the Lake and McHenry Plank Road. The produce arriving by wagon on what is now Belvidere Street came from western Lake County—for storage or for sale in the village or export by the lake. Banks were needed to facilitate this growing commerce, and toward the end of 1852 two other banks were established in Waukegan. One was short lived. The other, the Bank of Northern Illinois, merged in 1857 with C.R. and R. Steele. In the spring of 1989 the bank returned once again to its former name, The Bank of Northern

Illinois, N.A.

On March 10, 1865, the bank applied for and received a national bank charter. It began operation under its new charter as The First National Bank of Waukegan on Monday, April 17, 1865, just eight days after the end of the Civil War and two days after the death of Abraham Lincoln.

With the death of the bank's president, Charles Steele, in 1888, the pioneer era was largely over. The city was poised for industrialization. A beltline railroad was constructed, resulting in an influx of large manufacturing companies. Members of the Steele family continued to direct the bank's activities.

The "modern" era of The First National Bank of Waukegan began with the construction of new quarters in 1925. Standing at the city's busiest intersection, Washington and Genesee streets, the bank extends convenient and dependable service to the public in a wide variety of financial matters.

The bank is owned by the First Waukegan Corporation, which purchased it from the Steele family in 1979.

In 1852, shortly after the town of Little Fort became Waukegan, The First National Bank of Waukegan was established in this building, which was used from 1852 to 1861.

The principal stockholders in the First Waukegan Corporation, Harry J. Bystricky and Raymond A. Eiden, recognized the great potential of a financial institution at the doorstep of a newly expanding recreational area and whose commercial development would be enhanced by the potential industrial and residential growth projections for northeastern Illinois.

The First National Bank of Waukegan has enjoyed record growth and prosperity since it was acquired by the new investment team. It must achieve to survive in a changing marketplace that also must cope with the expansion of the major money center banks into Lake and Cook counties. New technology and systems, and continuous skill and product training are constantly provided to meet the needs and demands of the rapidly changing economic environment.

The bank has expanded from its Waukegan base. After a test of the market in 1985, the bank built a 15,000-square-foot, full-service center in Gurnee in May 1987. Gurnee is one of the fastest growing business and industrial communities adjacent to the northwest corner of Waukegan. The bank also has a facility in Libertyville.

Today's economic environment has resulted in more complex financial needs for both the commercial and retail customer, and The First National Bank of Waukegan is pledged to continually strive to meet those needs.

The main office of The First National Bank of Waukegan as it appears today. Major renovation took place in the spring of 1989.

THE KEMPER GROUP

The Kemper Group has called Lake County home since it moved its corporate headquarters to Long Grove in November 1971. A leading competitor in the insurance and financial services business worldwide, the company now employs roughly 2,400 of its more than 16,600-member staff there.

Organized in Chicago in 1912 as a single mutual workers' compensation insurer, Kemper today writes most types of personal and commercial property-casualty insurance. Known for its financial strength and high claim-handling standards, Kemper's property-casualty companies have led the way in innovations such as insurance coverage for industrial robots and repair/replacement coverage for cars. Kemper is the 17th-largest property-casualty insurer group in the country.

The organization now also includes three other major business segments—life insurance, reinsurance, and investment services—each among the leaders in its field.

Kemper's life insurance companies

About 2,400 employees work at The Kemper Group's international headquarters in Long Grove. The complex encompasses 620 acres, including five interconnecting lakes.

have more than a half-million policyholders, with insurance and annuities worth more than $51 billion; Kemper Reinsurance Company is the 14th-largest professional reinsurer in the United States; the Kemper network of securities broker-dealers comprises the 11th-largest force of registered representatives in the United States; and Kemper Financial Services is Chicago's largest money manager.

Kemper's Long Grove complex is on a 620-acre site. The grounds contain more than 200 different varieties of trees, flowers, and shrubs. To preserve the natural environment, none of the buildings was constructed more than

three stories high.

Five connecting man-made lakes border the buildings on three sides. The largest covers 68 acres and is a half-mile long. Hundreds of ducks and geese and a small flock of white swans make their home around the lakes.

The 18-hole championship Kemper Lakes Golf Course wraps around the company's complex and serves as the home of the Illinois Professional Golf Association. It is also the annual site of the Grand Slam of Golf and the 1989 PGA Championship. The course, along with the Kemper Lakes Tennis Club, operates as an independent profit center and is open to the public. A physical fitness trail, consisting of 18 exercise stations over a 1.5-mile course, also preserves the natural surroundings of Kemper's site.

Kemper is proud of its home in Lake County and strives to do its share as a good corporate neighbor. The company actively supports a variety of community programs, especially in the areas of health, safety, and youth. This support takes the form of financial assistance, in-kind donations such as printing and meeting space, as well as volunteers. The company-sponsored Junior Achievement program, for instance, has involved thousands of Lake County young people in running their own businesses with the guidance of Kemper employee volunteer consultants.

The Kemper Group congratulates Lake County on its 150th anniversary and looks forward to many more years of mutual growth and prosperity.

The Kemper Lakes Golf Course, open to the public, is consistently rated as one of the country's top golf courses. Kemper Lakes, the site of the Grand Slam of Golf, will host the 1989 PGA Championship.

FIRST MIDWEST BANCORP, INC.

The First Midwest Bank is a modern, flourishing institution with roots deep into Lake County. The bank was founded in 1908 in Zion, Illinois, as the First State Bank of Zion City. It became a national institution in 1936 and changed its name to Citizens National Bank of Waukegan.

First Midwest Bancorp, Inc., is headquartered in Waukegan, and with recent growth and expansion into Lake County, First Midwest is now the largest financial institution in the county.

The bank opened its first branch in 1944 at Great Lakes Naval Training Center to serve the large wartime recruit population. The following year Citizens National Bank joined forces with Union National Bank and Trust Company of Joliet to form what, four decades later, has become First Midwest Bancorp, Inc.

The bank undertook a major remodeling of the lobby facilities in 1955; but by 1963 additional facilities were needed. Five new drive-in windows, a customer parking lot, and the 19 North County Building were constructed.

The 216 Washington Street Building was purchased in 1964 to accommodate expansion needs, renovated two years later, and in 1972 the six-story building at 214 Washington Street was purchased. In 1974 a freestanding facility was built at the corner of Spaulding and Buckley roads to house the branch at Great Lakes. In 1981 the Northside office at 1201 Golf Road was completed.

A major change took place in 1983, when Citizens Bank and 19 other institutions joined to form First Midwest Bancorp, Inc., a multibank holding company. First Midwest's assets were $1.4 billion, making it the largest banking organization outside of Chicago and the sixth largest in Illinois.

From 1984 to 1988 the growth and expansion of First Midwest Bancorp into Lake County included the purchase of the Bank of Mundelein, the National Bank of North Chicago, the Continental Bank of Deerfield, the Bank of Zion, and the Midwest National Bank of Lake Forest, making First Midwest the largest financial institution in the county, with assets of $540 million as of June 1988.

First Midwest classifies its financial services into seven basic needs, which helps customers to focus on personal situations rather than the banking services available. The seven needs—all satisfied at the bank—include:

Managing cash. This need is generally satisfied through the use of checking accounts, money market accounts, automatic funds transfers, direct deposits, automatic teller banking, and home banking.

Managing debt. This task can often be linked to the checking account, which facilitates the payment of credit accounts (monthly credit payments, automatic debits) and allows a customer access to lines of credit.

Managing savings. In some cases, savings requirements can also be made easier through the checking account—a payroll deduction into a savings account is only one way to accomplish this goal. In addition to passbook savings, other savings instruments include certificates of deposit, individual retirement accounts, and Keogh accounts.

Managing investments. Along with CDs and IRAs, investing needs include using trust and investment accounts, as well as using a discount brokerage service for buying and selling mutual funds, stocks, and bonds.

Tax planning. Such tasks include assistance with preparation of returns, sheltering income, and financial planning for tax strategies.

Estate planning. This need is primarily satisfied through the use of trusts, as well as the writing of wills or other instruments to ensure the smooth transfer of assets.

Protection of assets. This can be assured by using personal insurance of various types. Another form of asset protection includes the use of safe deposit boxes for the safekeeping of stocks, bonds, and wills.

HEWITT ASSOCIATES

Hewitt Associates, the international benefit and compensation consulting firm, is fast approaching its 50th anniversary. For all but 10 of those 50 years the firm has been headquartered in Lake County. The company's first office was located in Lake Forest, Illinois. Later offices were located in Chicago, Libertyville, and Deerfield. In 1978 the firm relocated to its current 43-acre headquarters on Half Day Road in Lincolnshire.

The firm has experienced tremendous growth over the years. Until 1959 Hewitt Associates provided all services out of one office. Today it operates from 48 offices in 14 countries worldwide, and employs more than 2,000 associates.

Founded in 1940 by Edwin Shields Hewitt, the firm originally provided financial and estate planning consulting services to executives, but shifted direction within a few years to focus primarily on providing employee benefit design services for companies. As the benefit field has changed and become increasingly complex, the role of Hewitt Associates has expanded. To-

day the firm's consultants and actuaries specialize in all aspects of employee benefits and compensation, including design, financing, communication, and administration.

The areas in which the firm consults are far reaching and continually expanding. In the early 1970s Hewitt Associates pioneered the concept of flexible compensation—one of the fastest growing approaches to delivering employee benefits and compensation. Flexible programs offer choices among different benefits—helping employers to control the escalating cost of benefit programs, and allowing employees to select the types of benefits and levels of coverage that best meet their individual needs.

Hewitt Associates also has become a recognized leader in the development of computer software for benefit administration—currently one of the highest growth areas of the business. The firm offers a broad range of software products and services for the administration of pension, profit-sharing and other defined contribution arrangements; flexible compensation; and salary administration programs.

Hewitt Associates has been recognized for its unique operating style. The firm uses a team approach to con-

Edwin Shields Hewitt soon after the founding of the business in 1940.

sulting. Professional group consultants who specialize in different benefit and compensation disciplines—such as actuarial science, benefit administration, executive compensation, and salary administration—support account managers who are responsible for overall management of client projects and relationships. The firm operates as an extension of the client staff, helping to identify problems, consider alternatives, make decisions, and implement ideas.

From the outset, the focus at Hewitt Associates has been on delivering quality service. Hence, the people providing that service are of the utmost importance. The firm takes a long-term view of each associate's career development—striving to develop the potential within each person and find the best fit for them within the organization. The firm also encourages feedback from employees regarding the work environment. In recognition of its policies, Hewitt Associates received mention in two recent books—*The 100 Best Companies to Work for in America* (1985) and *The Best Companies for Women* (1988).

The Lincolnshire headquarters of Hewitt Associates, located at 100 Half Day Road.

STACK-ON PRODUCTS

The formula to build a flourishing, internationally known, and competitive company is no secret. All it takes is unending seven-day weeks, around-the-clock days, and a stubborn determination to never fail. Just ask John Lynn how it is done. He is the president and owner of Stack-On Products. And together with George Fenzke, who is now retired, the two men built the company.

Today Stack-On Products manufactures and sells steel toolboxes, rollaway tool cabinets, and related equipment nationwide and in Europe. The cabinets are sturdy, durable, and functional.

But in the beginning there was only the idea—a concept for the design of metal toolboxes. There were no customers and there was no money. There was, however, the challenge to create and to build.

Stack-On Products was incorporated July 1, 1972, and started production of steel toolboxes in January 1973 in Round Lake. The firm was located in the old Creamery Building, where Lake County farmers once made cream. It began as a job shop primarily. In addition to tool cabinets, it also produced animal cages, a product line it has since dropped.

Attending the ribbon-cutting ceremony for the new Stack-On Products plant in Wauconda in 1983 are (from left) George Fenzke, then chairman of the board of Stack-On Products, now retired; Glenn Miller, chairman of the Lake County Board and representative for District 6; and John Lynn, president and chief executive officer of Stack-On Products.

The original Creamery Building where Stack-On Products was started.

The firm came into being shortly after Fenzke had retired from the company he had owned. Lynn had been the plant manager there, but he was looking for new avenues to explore. He suggested that he and Fenzke join forces, and that is how Stack-On Products came to be.

At first, the production team consisted of Lynn and his two teenage sons. The three of them machined parts and assembled the tool cabinets. Fenzke functioned as the company's sales force. He traveled through most of the states east of the Mississippi River hunting for customers. He found them, too.

Stack-On Products was successful in bidding for government business from the General Services Administration. It was awarded a substantial contract in 1973. With the signing of the GSA contract, Stack-On Products began its consistent, upward pattern of growth that continues to this day.

The GSA contract was also important because it provided the revenue with which to purchase more modern, labor-saving equipment. Until then, most of the work involved in making Stack-On Products' cabinets had been largely manual, which inhibited the rapid and efficient production of larger quantities of goods.

In 1974 Stack-On Products purchased the buildings in which it was located and had been renting. The company expanded its facilities, and installed a conveyorized paint system.

Stack-On Products continued to flourish and grow during this period, and a major power tool corporation was signed on as an important customer. That relationship, as well as the one with GSA, continues to this day.

The company also manufactures

cabinets for the original equipment market, making tool boxes to the specifications of other corporations. Since the firm's inception, the OEM segment has been an important aspect of Stack-On Products' business.

As business grew, sales were expanded by the creation of an extensive network of sales representatives that now reaches across the United States. A sales manager was hired in 1982 to direct the network. The firm began selling in Europe in the early 1980s and now has direct sales people in Europe.

Stack-On Products believes in listening closely to the purchasers of its goods to see what they want and need. The company also is represented at trade shows to heighten its visibility and to keep abreast of what is happening in the industry. In Europe, Stack-On Products is represented at the trade fairs in Cologne and Frankfurt. All of

boxes, chests, and cabinets. Stack-On tool-storage systems provide all levels of professionals with the durability, convenience, and security they need to store, organize, and protect their valuable tools and equipment.

The modular design of the firm's cabinets allows the professional to expand his Stack-On system as his tool-storage needs grow. All Stack-On chests, rollaways, and accessory units are versatile, allowing the customer a choice of add-on components without having to buy an entirely new system.

From the beginning Stack-On Products has never failed to grow each year that it has been in business.

Upon Fenzke's retirement in 1986,

This new 64,000-square-foot plant in Wauconda marks the second stage of the company's growth. Photo taken in 1983.

the firm's European importers also appear at trade shows in their individual countries.

In 1982 the growing organization began construction of its present facilities in Wauconda. This new structure consists of 64,000 square feet of modern offices and manufacturing space, and was occupied in 1983. An additional 40,000-square-foot warehouse was added in March 1987.

Currently Stack-On Products manufactures a variety of steel tool-

all of his responsibilities were assumed by Lynn, who is now president and chief executive officer. His expertise continues to be in manufacturing and products design, although, with the growth of the operation, he has delegated duties in these areas. Lynn continues to handle the accounts of the firm's major customers.

Since it was founded, Stack-On Products has taken an active interest in the affairs of its community. Fenzke served for five years as the president of

the Round Lake Chamber of Commerce, and Lynn is a director of the Wauconda chamber.

Stack-On Products is interested in the development of young people. The company hires young men and women from all over Lake County, and it does not require them to have had previous experience. While Lynn supervised training of new hires when the firm was small, Stack-On Products now has its own training programs.

Many of the current managers in responsible positions came to the company without any previous skills or experience. In this capacity, Stack-On Products is proud of its role as a starting ground for local young people.

Stack-On Products is one of the major employers in Lake County. Many employees who helped start the firm are still with it. Its move into the community of Wauconda served as a catalyst for a boom in local development.

Today Stack-On Products looks to the future with confidence. The company anticipates expanding its markets while continuing to build on a reputation of customer satisfaction and quality manufacturing.

Stage three of Stack-On Products' growth was completed in 1987 with this 104,000-square-foot plant in the center of a Wauconda industrial park.

OUTBOARD MARINE CORPORATION

Outboard Marine Corporation (OMC) is a leader in the manufacturing and marketing of marine products and services, consumer and commercial turf-care equipment, and light commercial vehicles. A number of OMC brands, such as Johnson Outboards, Evinrude Outboards, OMC Cobra Stern Drives, Four Winns boats, Stratos bass boats, Lawn-Boy lawn-care products, and Cushman vehicles, are among the most widely recognized and respected brand names in their industries.

In 1987 OMC ranked 269th on *Fortune* magazine's listing of the 500 largest industrial corporations in the United States, up 37 places from the year before.

Headquartered in Waukegan, OMC manufactures products for the world in 23 U.S. plants and six international facilities. It employs almost 12,000 individuals worldwide.

OMC today makes boats as well as marine engines. After careful analysis of the growing trend toward one-stop shopping by marine dealers and customers, OMC entered the boat-manufacturing business in 1986. Between December 1986 and early 1988, OMC purchased six boat companies and added the following brand names: Four Winns, Lowe, Stratos, Sunbird, Seaswirl, and Sea Nymph. These firms were selected because they were fast growing, profitable, aggressively managed, and had a high-quality image in

The 1989 Johnson GT® 300.

the marketplace.

OMC Adventurent, Inc., a boat rental operation, is another means of attracting new customers to OMC marine products. With 35 outlets in Florida, California, Texas, Georgia, and Ohio, Adventurent allows boaters to conveniently sample recreational marine products.

OMC has also launched a retail venture designed to reach out to new boaters. Called Top of the Dock, Inc., the stores will be opened in conjunction with local OMC dealers in high-volume shopping malls where demographics closely match those of first-time buyers.

OMC's power lawn products group has embarked on a program to transform it from a single-line supplier of walk-behind rotary-powered mowers into a full-line manufacturer of outdoor power equipment. Lawn-Boy's line now includes rear-engine riding mowers and lawn and garden tractors, two of the industry's fastest-growing product categories, as well as garden tillers and snow throwers. It also makes the Sensation line of commercial mowers, designed for use by professional

lawn-maintenance services.

OMC's sales of vehicles and turf-care equipment continue to increase. Its well-known brands are Cushman and Ryan. Brouwer Turf Equipment, Ltd., the world's leading manufacturer of sod-harvesting equipment, was acquired in 1986.

OMC believes product innovation is an important ingredient in sales success. One such recent development is the Ryan Mataway Overseeder, a special attachment for the Ryan Mataway power rake. Together the units allow an operator to dethatch and reseed a turf area in a single operation.

The College and University Turf Equipment Program has grown dramatically. This program, administered by dealers, provides free use of Ryan and Cushman equipment to educational institutions with horticulture, landscape, and turfgrass programs.

Internationally, Outboard Marine Corporation has the most extensive worldwide distribution system in the marine industry. The company is using the strength of this system to support its sales of outboards, stern drives, boats, and accessories through carefully developed international programs.

Ralph Evinrude and S.F. Briggs, founders of Outboard Marine Corporation, are pictured in this photograph taken sometime in the 1930s.

BANK OF WAUKEGAN

The Bank of Waukegan's Main Office, at 1601 North Lewis Avenue, was founded in 1962.

The Bank of Waukegan is a state-chartered bank that was founded in 1962. The doors first opened for business on November 2, 1962, at 1601 North Lewis Avenue, the present site of the Bank of Waukegan's Main Office. In June 1980 the institution's Westside Facility was opened at Green Bay Road and Grand Avenue, and in April 1983 the Antioch Facility opened at Route 59 at Grass Lake Road. The bank's purpose is to effectively serve the business and personal financial needs of the people of northern Lake County.

The Bank of Waukegan is a wholly owned subsidiary of Northern States Financial Corporation (NSFC). NSFC is also the parent company for another subsidiary, Northern States Trust Company, which is located on the second floor of the Westside Facility. The Westside Facility was remodeled from the shell of the former Spaulding School, and also houses several condominium offices in the structure's former classrooms.

Northern States Trust Company, which moved from Antioch to Waukegan in January 1986, specializes in trust and investment services with an added emphasis on employee benefit plans for small businesses. It was formed to provide access to financial services typically not offered by banking organizations and has experienced rapid growth in the past few years. It also administers individual trusts and provides specialized investment services for individuals, corporations, and municipalities.

The Bank of Waukegan has been successful in maintaining a well-balanced mix of retail, commercial, and real estate business, and provides every conceivable type of account for its customers. The bank specializes in working with small to medium-size businesses and offers installment, commercial, and real estate loans.

Many of the bank's officers and employees have a number of years of service with the institution, a feature that provides the kind of stability customers appreciate. Because customers today are more sophisticated in the ways they use banking services, the in-

The Bank of Waukegan Westside Facility at Green Bay Road and Grand Avenue on the former Spaulding School site.

stitution's goal is to serve their needs in the most cost-efficient manner possible.

The institution was the first bank in Waukegan to offer automated teller machines and is considered a leader in providing electronic banking services. It is a member of both the prestigious Cash Station Automated Teller Network in the Chicagoland area and the nationwide CIRRUS network.

To ensure a continuing high level of service and professional competency, the bank has a well-structured and ongoing employee training program. It is this blend of careful training and career longevity that produces effective service and satisfied, long-term customers.

The bank is also community-minded and supports a wide variety of civic and cultural activities and events. Its sponsorship of the Annual Lake County Marathon/10K Race has helped make that run one of the premier sports events in the Midwest. It also participates in a number of parades, trade shows, and professional organizations.

The Bank of Waukegan is optimistic about its future and the future of Lake County. Population growth and increasing residential and commercial construction have resulted in a healthy and vigorous business climate and increasing loan demand. The Bank of Waukegan has the resources, expertise, and professional competence to aggressively promote that growth and continue to meet the needs of its customers.

BAXTER INTERNATIONAL INC.

For more than a half-century Baxter International Inc. has worked to improve the lives of people worldwide—patients undergoing surgery and diagnostic testing, soldiers injured in combat, the elderly and infirm, accident and burn victims, those suffering from cancer and heart disease, and patients in the hospital and patients at home. Baxter's commitment has always been to caring, to quality, and to innovation.

Today intravenous solutions are used routinely. Prior to 1931, however, many patients died from dehydration and malnutrition, or from pyrogens present in the early hospital-made solutions. Baxter was founded in 1931 for the express purpose of finding ways to make intravenous therapy safe; the company's solutions were the first to ensure absolute purity.

In 1956 Baxter pioneered the first commercially built dialysis machine, a technology that evolved from a prototype made of orange-juice cans and washing-machine parts. Dialysis machines now help more than 300,000 victims of kidney disease live productive lives.

In the late 1930s Baxter also turned its attention to blood therapy. At that time, collected blood could be stored for only a few hours, and a suitable donor had to be available whenever a transfusion was needed. Often the process was too slow to save the patient's life. In 1939 Baxter introduced the first sterile, pyrogen-free system to draw and administer blood. Each bottle contained an anticoagulant, which allowed the blood to be stored safely for up to three weeks and "banked" for future use.

Another breakthrough came in 1941, when Baxter found a way to separate plasma from red blood cells. Unlike whole blood, plasma could be stored almost indefinitely. The discovery came when the need was greatest. During World War II the American military used more than one million Baxter blood packs and 4 million bottles of Baxter intravenous solutions to save young lives.

Another new life-saving medical specialty evolved from little more than orange juice cans and washing machine parts. This unlikely contraption led to the development of the first commercially manufactured kidney dialysis

Baxter International Inc. merged with American Hospital Supply Corporation in 1985 to become the world's largest supplier of health care products. The multinational corporation employs 60,000 people in 29 countries and is headquartered in Deerfield.

system, introduced by Baxter in 1956. Today more than 300,000 people worldwide owe their lives to this technological breakthrough, and to the new self-administered dialysis therapy pioneered by Baxter in recent years.

As medical science began to explore the area of open-heart surgery, Baxter worked with renowned heart surgeons Drs. Michael DeBakey and Denton Cooley to develop the first disposable oxygenator to perform the function of the heart and lungs during cardiovascular surgery. Today Baxter heart valves, diagnostic catheters, and cardiac bypass systems are keeping thousands of patients alive and well.

In 1968 Baxter made another dramatic contribution to medicine with the introduction of Antihemophilic Factor Concentrate, an effective and practical treatment for hemophilia. Prior to that time, patients required massive transfusions of plasma that sometimes overloaded the circulatory system. Many young patients died or were left severely crippled.

Baxter merged with American Hospital Supply Corporation in 1985 to become the world's largest supplier of health care products. Today annual sales exceed $6 billion. The multinational corporation employs 60,000 people in 29 countries and is headquartered in Deerfield.

Baxter is meeting the challenges of a changing health care environment through products and services that help hospitals increase productivity and reduce costs, and through new technologies that help providers deliver high-quality care to patients in a variety of settings, from hospital to home.

Today Baxter offers the broadest line of hospital products and services in the industry, satisfying more than 65 percent of a hospital's needs. Its advanced distribution and computer systems help hospitals to purchase and manage supplies more efficiently.

Baxter's research and technological capabilities contribute to almost every area of health care. It develops, markets, and improves manufacturing processes for blood and diagnostic therapies, medical specialties devices, cardiac care equipment, and laboratory supplies.

Baxter's home care affords high-quality, life-sustaining therapies for those with cancer and other diseases. Health-cost management offers mail-order prescriptions, utilization review, case management, and cost analysis to businesses, government, and third-party payers. Distribution services provide medical supplies to doctors' offices, surgicenters, nursing homes, and other alternate-site locations.

About 21 percent of Baxter's sales are outside the United States. The company's products are manufactured in 20 countries and sold in more than 100 nations. The breadth of the firm's manufacturing and marketing network affords a competitive edge in penetrat-

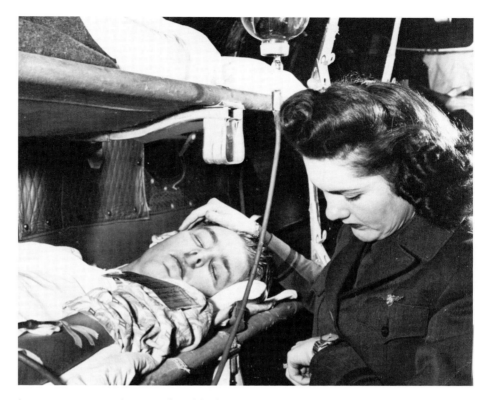

ing overseas markets and achieving leadership.

Baxter's Global Businesses Group has four international research and development centers in Belgium, Germany, Australia, and Japan. These centers provide critical links with university and other medical researchers worldwide.

Baxter's Systems Division, a pioneer in the integration of clinical and financial data, provides computer-based systems to help health care providers control costs and manage clinical information.

Using IBM-based technology, the Systems Division offers complete software products for every size hospital to automate financial, administrative, and patient care tasks. For clients who require ongoing support, the division provides consulting and contract services, including product management, capacity planning, data center engineering, and construction and facility management.

Corporate Sales provides large

An American soldier during World War II receives intravenous medication in a plane somewhere over the Pacific. Baxter's IV solutions and blood collection products were the first to meet armed forces specifications.

hospitals, medical centers, multihospital systems, and purchasing groups with a single point of contact to gain immediate and easy access to all of the corporation's products, services, and systems.

The Distribution Division assures the delivery of the corporation's products through a unique facility and transportation network.

Baxter International Inc. understands that it takes a lot more than products to meet the real needs of hospitals, physicians, and patients. It takes dedication and the ability to provide unequaled service. It takes a recognition that Baxter's success is dependent on its customers' success. Only by working together as partners can Baxter and its customers provide cost-effective health care.

HOLIDAY INN, GURNEE

The Holiday Inn of Gurnee, located at the intersection of Interstate 94 and Route 132 (Grand Avenue), was opened for guests in July 1970. The original building cost $1.5 million and contained 113 guest rooms, more than 3,500 square feet of meeting and banquet space, a restaurant-lounge, and an outdoor swimming pool.

Successful from its inception, the guest list grew even longer in 1976 after Marriott Corporation opened Great America, its huge family amusement park, nearby.

Ever alert to its guests' comfort, Holiday Inn, Gurnee, completed an extensive, $2-million remodeling program in 1984. A new recreation building with an indoor heated pool, whirlpool, poolside snack shop, and an electronic game arcade and Zackery's, a new restaurant and show lounge, were created, along with a high-ceiling atrium for receptions. All 113 guest rooms were completely refurbished, as was the main lobby and ballroom. Five new conference rooms, for a total of 1,080 square feet, were added.

In 1988 a new, four-story addition was constructed to add another 112 guest rooms for a total of 225. This new wing cost $3.5 million.

In addition to the standard, two-

The Holiday Inn, Gurnee, went through an extensive $2-million remodeling program in 1984. The main lobby, pictured here, was completely refurbished.

As part of the remodeling program this greenhouse was added to Zackery's Restaurant for a fresh new look.

bedded rooms and King Leisure rooms that are spacious enough for work and entertaining, this new wing features six rooms designed for handicapped travelers, two conference rooms, two conference/hospitality suites, a non-smoking floor, four deluxe king rooms, and an executive floor for corporate travelers. The Executive Floor features free use of an executive lounge with cocktails and appetizers in the evening, and buffet breakfast in the morning.

The comfort of a full-service, luxury hotel is the kind of leadership guests expect from the largest hotel chain in the world.

Holiday Inn, Gurnee, is a participant in the Holidex reservation system—a guest can reserve a room in any Holiday Inn in the world from the inn in which he or she is staying.

There is a long list of amenities available to every guest: a free cup of coffee and newspaper delivered to the room with a requested wake-up call; the pool, hot tub, and game room open from 7 a.m. to midnight every day; free appetizers in Zackery's lounge, 4 to 6 p.m., weekdays; complimentary daily

newspapers at the front desk; free shuttle transportation within the immediate area for groups of 10; a valet service that offers same-day laundry and dry-cleaning service; samples of razors, shaving cream, hair spray, and other such items to guests who may have forgotten something; a clock radio, remote-control television, and free ESPN, CNN, and Showtime cable channels in every room; and a coin laundry.

One reason Holiday Inn, Gurnee, is flourishing is that it is in the center of growing Lake County. Lake County is attracting many new businesses, and there has been a home-building boom in recent years. The inn is in the center of this market and on a north-south tourist route.

In addition, the inn is close to downtown Chicago, O'Hare International Airport, downtown Milwaukee, and Mitchell Field. Greyhound bus service is available directly to the hotel from O'Hare and Mitchell Field. Close by are shopping centers, golf courses, Chain-of-Lakes, and Lake Michigan.

The Holiday Inn, Gurnee, is a franchise owned and operated by Gurnee Inns, Inc. The president is Sherman St. Pierre of Antioch and the vice-president is Jack Koslow of Skokie. Richard Hedden is the general manager.

WKRS/WXLC

Program director Nick Farella (right) and promotions director Mark West proudly introduce the new WXLC Music Power remote van with pneumatic mast for long-distance broadcasting.

Residents of Lake County or those driving through who want to listen either to the most recent news or to good music have only to tune to WKRS AM 1220 or WXLC FM 102.3 stereo.

WKRS is an adult radio station. It primarily programs news, sports, and information, including radio talk shows, to a target audience of listeners between the ages of 25 and 54. For discussions on the most recent issues in the news, listeners tune in during the morning hours; for other topics of interest to Lake County listeners, listeners switch on during the afternoon hours when the talk format is less structured.

During the morning drive-time every hour is filled with 60 minutes of news and information. WKRS is affiliated with the ABC Direction Network for live satellite-delivered news service, as well as the Associated Press newswire. It is also the official weather bureau reporting station for the Waukegan area.

WKRS' sister station, WXLC, programs CHR (contemporary hit radio) music to a target audience ranging in age from 18 to 49, emphasizing those from 18 to 34.

WKRS has been a public servant to the residents of Lake County since 1949. The WKRS radio audience is composed primarily of listeners in northern Illinois and southern Wisconsin. These listeners know that WKRS is a primary source of daily local information. In fact, a strong emphasis on locally oriented news has been a tradition with WKRS since its founding by Frank Just, the publisher of the *Waukegan News-Sun*. The station today, however, is not affiliated with the newspaper. Both WKRS and WXLC are owned by Hartstone and Dickstein Inc., an investment group out of Hartford, Connecticut.

WKRS initially signed on the air as an FM station in July 1948. It turned up on the FM dial because the license-granting procedure was quicker for FM than it was for AM in the late 1940s. The present station, WKRS AM, signed on in September 1949. The FM signal was too far ahead of its time to gain adequate public acceptance or advertiser support, and in 1952 the FM station went dead, the license returned to the FCC. In those days public eyes were turned toward that new toy, television. It was not until many years later that radio listeners began to appreciate the fidelity of FM sound.

WKRS did not team up again with an FM station until a previous WKRS owner, Roger Kaplan, bought an FM station in Waukegan and joined it with WKRS in 1983. Kaplan sold the stations to the present ownership in the fall of 1987.

WXLC is currently directly between Chicago and Milwaukee on the Lake Michigan shoreline, with a 24-hour signal that is listenable for more than 35 miles west to Woodstock in central McHenry County. While the primary signal area is almost totally Lake County, additional listeners within the station's strongest signal area live on Chicago's North Shore and South Shore in Wisconsin.

WXLC is the most visible station in the market. It enhances its appeal to its advertisers by going to them with its exclusive "Traveling Radio Show," with personalities, a TV-type set, broadcast truck, and giveaways. WXLC is also the number-one station in the market for contests.

Both WKRS and WXLC operate with a new, state-of-the-art production studio with multichannel capability. In 1988 more than $100,000 was spent for capital improvements to upgrade the broadcast facility. And to increase visibility and flexibility, a new remote broadcast vehicle has been purchased for WXLC.

WKRS/WXLC news director Dan Keeney (left) on location at a developing story for the News-1220 team.

ABBOTT LABORATORIES

In 1888 a 30-year-old neighborhood physician named Wallace Calvin Abbott began making new medicines in his home on Chicago's North Side. Abbott Laboratories has since evolved into a major multinational health care company with business in pharmaceuticals, nutritionals, hospital products, and diagnostics. One of the 100 largest American corporations on the *Fortune* 500 list, Abbott's sales in 1988 were $4.9 billion.

In the 1920s Abbott's operations were moved to Lake County. The company's headquarters is now located at Abbott Park, a 400-acre site some 40 miles north of Chicago. Its largest manufacturing facility is in the city of North Chicago, five miles northeast of the headquarters complex. At the end of 1987 Abbott owned and occupied more than 90 buildings—with more than 5.5 million square feet of floor space—in Lake County, with several additional facilities under construction. The firm has 24 other facilities in the United States, and manufacturing and distribution operations and joint ventures in more than 40 countries worldwide.

Of Abbott's 39,000 employees worldwide, nearly 10,000 work in Lake

Abbott Park, the company's world headquarters, is located at the intersection of Buckley and Waukegan roads in Lake County.

County, making Abbott the county's largest private employer. Abbott's share of local and state taxes—together with taxes paid by Abbott employees, retirees, and suppliers—support many essential social programs and services in the area. Abbott itself spends more than $40 million to purchase goods and services from other Lake County businesses.

Abbott has grown by developing cost-effective products, technologies, and services that improve health care worldwide. In the 1930s the company developed Pentothal, the largest-selling intravenous anesthetic in the world, and sulfanilamide, the first of the "miracle drugs." In the 1940s Abbott produced dried blood plasma for the armed forces and was one of the early pioneers in penicillin production. In the 1950s the firm developed Erythrocin—one of the safest and most widely used antibiotics today.

A 1964 merger brought the Similac line of infant formula to Abbott. New products in the 1970s included Tranxene for anxiety, Ausria to detect hepatitis, Abbokinase for pulmonary embolism, and Depakene for epilepsy.

An Abbott diagnostic test to screen blood for antibodies to the AIDS virus, introduced in 1985, was the first approved by the U.S. government. Abbott is the leader in the worldwide diagnostics market.

In 1987 the firm donated more than $450,000 to United Way agencies and nonprofit organizations in Lake County and an additional $175,000 to Chicago-area civic and cultural organizations. Abbott matches employees' contributions (more than $500,000 in 1987) to institutions of higher learning, hospitals, and nonpublic secondary schools. The company awards scholarships to graduating seniors from four Lake County high schools, and the Clara Abbott Foundation awards roughly 2,000 educational grants each year to children of employees and retirees.

The company also donates medical supplies and drug products to people in poverty-stricken areas and disaster sites worldwide. Product donations totaled $5.1 million at cost in 1987.

Abbott Laboratories has benefited from its location in Lake County, and the company's growth and economic success, and the talents and community dedication of its employees and retirees have helped the region prosper as a major commercial and residential area.

Dr. Wallace Calvin Abbott, company founder, used a single-row horse-drawn plow during the ground-breaking ceremony for the North Chicago plant in 1920.

MARRIOTT'S LINCOLNSHIRE RESORT

Marriott's Lincolnshire Resort is a complete resort hotel on 170 wooded acres on Chicago's North Shore. The 400-room resort is an oasis in a rapidly urbanizing area. Its serenity is doubly ensured: It is the only major hotel in Lake County that is not located within 100 feet of a major expressway.

Opened in 1975, Marriott's Lincolnshire Resort is multifaceted, offering theater-in-the-round, meeting and convention facilities, recreation and sports facilities for weekend guests, and a place for weddings, bar mitzvahs, bas mitzvahs, and other personal occasions for families and organizations. A three-member social staff works full time arranging these special occasions.

The resort has had a strong cultural impact in Lake County. Up to 5,000 patrons come to watch the eight weekly performances of highly popular plays and musicals offered in the 900-seat theater. There are also a variety of restaurants and lounges.

The resort's primary purpose is to serve as a meeting and convention facility. Marriott's Lincolnshire Resort caters to incentive and sales meetings, and it is especially suited for those businesses that are searching for a hotel that has recreational facilities.

There is an 18-hole golf course, a Racquet Club with indoor tennis and racquetball courts for year-round play,

The hotel offers a variety of recreation and sports facilities, including an 18-hole golf course, racquetball courts, indoor tennis, fully equipped health club, and indoor and outdoor swimming pools.

a fully equipped health club, as well as indoor and outdoor swimming pools. A new locker room with 175 lockers has recently been completed.

Almost every room on every level affords attractive views of the surrounding golf course or nearby woodlands. Amenities include king or double beds, AM/FM radio, and color TV with cable TV and free HBO, CNN, ESPN, and other current in-room movies. The resort is wheelchair accessible and barrier free. Five rooms have been especially equipped for handicapped guests.

Marriott's Lincolnshire Resort has 18,000 square feet of space for exhibitions and conventions. The highlight of the resort's 21 meeting rooms is the Grand Ballroom, the largest in Lake County with 10,080 square feet of divisible space. The ballroom comfortably accommodates groups of up to 1,500 for a reception, and 1,000 for a banquet or formal dinner. Smaller rooms, for groups of 50 to 150, can be created. Eight salons compose the Grand Ballroom, with smaller rooms ranging in size from 789 to 2,640

square feet. Retracting walls and combining salons allow for the creation of even more room.

The resort's in-house audiovisual team is well prepared to organize, equip, and set up an audiovisual presentation of any size. Sophisticated sound, projection and lighting equipment, plus state-of-the-art multimedia programming equipment are available for rental. The resort is also equipped for teleconferencing.

The catering staff will prepare a special theme party, buffet, or cocktail party that can be served under a colorful reception tent. The resort employs seven full-time staff members who work with a company to help plan its meeting from start to finish.

One of the keys to the resort's success is its easy accessibility to O'Hare International Airport. The resort is also popular with weekend guests from throughout the Midwest. Many guests like the rural setting and the resort's parklike campus. And because the resort is well located, guests can easily visit nearby attractions both in Lake County and in nearby Chicago.

With 700 employees, Marriott's Lincolnshire Resort is one of the largest employers in Lake County, and one of the largest providers of summer jobs for high school and college students. Every summer the resort also takes in 30 to 40 interns who are studying hotel management.

Located on 170 wooded acres on Chicago's North Shore, the 400-room Marriott's Lincolnshire Resort began operations in 1975.

LAKE FOREST HOSPITAL

Lake Forest Hospital was founded in 1899 with an initial donation of $5,000 from Mrs. Henry Clay Durant. Lake Forest then had a population of 2,000. Named the Alice Home in memory of Mrs. Durant's late sister, the hospital was located on the grounds of Lake Forest College and its special strength was maternity.

Lake Forest Hospital has enjoyed deep community support. From the beginning the outpouring of community financial support was prompt and generous.

For its first four decades, the Alice Home grew to meet the needs of the expanding town, but by the late 1930s it was clear that a new hospital would have to be built. Twenty-five acres of land for the new building were donated by the widow and son of Albert B. Dick. This parcel, which was on the then-western edge of town, was part of the Dick family's Westmoreland farm. It is the site of the present-day hospital, although the modern campus has grown beyond the original 25 acres.

A.B. Dick, Jr., and his mother were instrumental in getting the new hospital under way, and it was opened in 1942. They required the institution to have an all-specialist staff, physicians board certified in a specialty, and that remains true to this day.

As a not-for-profit community

The solarium at Westmoreland, an 82-resident long-term care facility on the hospital's campus.

Lake Forest Hospital's front exterior is reminiscent of a New England university.

hospital, Lake Forest Hospital is governed by a board of directors composed of members representing the community and the medical staff.

A feature of Lake Forest Hospital since its inception is that many members of the medical staff have been associated with other hospitals in the area, especially Rush and St. Luke's before those institutions merged into the present-day Rush-Presbyterian-St. Luke's complex.

In 1942, when the new building opened, it had 41 beds and 28 physicians. Today there are more than 240 physicians on the staff.

After the end of World War II a new era of growth began. Quarters for employees were constructed, and bed capacity grew to 101 in 1959. In 1967 beds numbered 161, and a cardiac and intensive care unit was opened. In 1968 an X-ray and radiation therapy center was opened and physical therapy was expanded. A cobalt machine was installed the following year.

Within the past 10 years Lake Forest Hospital has been totally renovated and expanded. It is now a full-service

hospital with a 160-acre campus.

Also on the campus is Westmoreland, an 82-resident long-term care facility that was opened in 1975. In addition to custodial care, Westmoreland provides residents with recreation and social opportunities. As a skilled nursing facility, Westmoreland offers physician coverage and professional nursing care 24 hours a day to meet the needs of residents with more complex health problems.

On campus there are also four physician office buildings and a conference center for community programs. Off campus, many services are provided at the hospital's Vernon Hills Medical Building at Butterfield Road, just north of Route 60.

Lake Forest Hospital has been designated by the Illinois Department of Public Health as a Level II trauma center, the first trauma center in Lake County.

Steady growth and development have helped Lake Forest Hospital serve the needs of more people in a growing number of communities throughout northern Illinois and southern Wisconsin. Yet the hospital's campus environment and the staff's dedication to quality have preserved the unique feature of highly effective personalized health care.

PATRONS

The following individuals, companies, and organizations have made a valuable commitment to the quality of this publication. Windsor Publications and the Waukegan/Lake County Chamber of Commerce gratefully acknowledge their participation in *Lake County, Illinois: This Land of Lakes and Rivers.*

Abbott Laboratories*
American National Bank of Libertyville*
Bank of Waukegan*
Baxter International Inc.*
Dexter Packaging and Specialty
    Coatings*
Fansteel*
First Midwest Bancorp, Inc.*
The First National Bank of Waukegan*
Goelitz Confectionery Company*
Good Shepherd Hospital*
Hewitt Associates*
Highland Park Hospital*
Holiday Inn, Gurnee*
Intrupa*
The Kemper Group*
Lake Forest Hospital*
Manville Sales Corp.*
Marriott's Lincolnshire Resort*
Meier's Masterbilt Manufacturing Home
    Leisure Centers*
North Shore Gas Company*
North Shore Savings and Loan
    Association*
NOSCO Inc.*
Outboard Marine Corporation*
Polyfoam Packers Corp.*
Stack-On Products*
The Travelodge*
UARCO*
Universal Outdoor Advertising*
University of Health Sciences/The
    Chicago Medical School*
Victory Memorial Hospital*
Walgreens*
WKRS/WXLC*

*Partners in Progress of *Lake County, Illinois: This Land of Lakes and Rivers.* The histories of these companies and organizations appear in Chapter 7, beginning on page 109.

BIBLIOGRAPHY

BOOKS AND ARTICLES

Arpee, Edward. *Lake Forest, Illinois: History and Reminiscences 1861-1961.* Lake Forest: Rotary Club of Lake Forest, 1963.

Bateman, Newton and Paul Selby. *Historical Encyclopedia of Illinois and History of Lake County.* Edited by Charles A. Partridge. Chicago: Munsell Publishing Co., 1902.

Benny, Mary Livingstone, and Hilliard Marks. *Jack Benny.* Garden City, New York: Doubleday & Company, Inc., 1978.

Berger, Philip, ed. *Highland Park American Suburb at Its Best.* Highland Park Landmark Preservation Committee, 1982.

Campbell, George V. *North Shore Line Memories.* Northbrook: Domus Books, 1980.

"Chicago History." *The Magazine of the Chicago Historical Society,* vol. 11, no. 2, 1982.

Clifton, James A. *The Prairie People.* Lawrence, Kansas: The Regents Press of Kansas, 1977.

Dorsey, Curtis. "Black Migration to Waukegan." In *Historical Highlights of the Waukegan Area,* edited by Louis and Julia Osling. The City of Waukegan, 1976.

Dorsey, James. *Up South.* N.p., n.d.

Ford, Dorothy L., comp. *Centennial Booklet of the First Congregational Church of Waukegan, Illinois.* 1943.

Greer, Ann L. *The Mayor's Mandate.* Cambridge, Massachusetts: Schenkman Publishing Company, 1974.

Gregory, Ruth, ed. *Waukegan Illinois Its Past, Its Present.* Waukegan: League of Women Voters and City of Waukegan, 1967.

Haines, Elijah M. *The American Indian.* Chicago: The Mas-sin-na-gan Company, 1888.

──────── . *Historical and Statistical Sketches of Lake County.* Waukegan: E.G. Howe, 1852.

Halsey, John J., ed. *A History of Lake County Illinois.* Chicago: Roy S. Bates, 1912.

Howard, Robert P. *Illinois—A History of the Prairie State.* Grand Rapids, Michigan: William B. Eerdmans Publishing Company, 1972.

Ivanhoe Origins: Key Events in the History of Ivanhoe Congregational Church. 1976.

Johnson, Jane Snodgrass. *History of Lake County with Biographies.* A Big-Little County History, 1939.

Knirsch, Roberta Selter. *The Town of Antioch: Its First Hundred Years.* Antioch: Trustees of the Antioch Township Library, 1987.

Kogan, Herman. *The Long White Line.* New York: Random House, 1963.

Lake County, Illinois 1980 Census Composite. Waukegan: Lake County Department of Planning, Zoning & Environmental Quality, 1987.

Lake Forest Art and History Edition. Chicago: American Communities Company, 1916.

Lake Villa Chamber of Commerce and Industry Publication. 1987.

Lindsay, Gordon. *The Life of John Alexander Dowie.* The Voice of Healing Publishing Company, 1951.

Manchester, William. *The Glory and the Dream.* Boston-Toronto: Little Brown and Company, 1973.

Martin, John Bartlow. *Adlai Stevenson of Illinois.* Garden City, New York: Doubleday & Company, Inc., 1976.

Mayer, S.L. "Forging a Nation 1866-1900." In *The Almanac of American History,* edited by Arthur M. Schlesinger, Jr. New York: The Putnam Publishing Group, 1983.

Meads, Joe. *How It All Began.* Compiled by the Lake Forest-Lake Bluff Historical Society, 1976.

Middleton, William D. *North Shore, America's Fastest Interurban.* San Marino, California: Golden West Books, 1964.

Mullery, Virginia. *Waukegan's Legacy Our Landmarks.* Waukegan: Waukegan Historical Society, 1979.

Partridge, Charles A., ed. *History of the Ninety-Sixth Regiment, Illinois Volunteer Infantry.* Chicago: Historical Society of the Regiment, 1887.

The Past and Present of Lake County, Ill. Chicago: William LeBaron & Company, 1877.

Portrait Biographical Album of Lake County Illinois. Chicago: Lake City Publishing Company, 1891.

Pratt, Richard. *David Adler, The Architect and His Work.* New York: M. Evans & Company, 1970.

Pratt, William D. *The Abbott Almanac.* Elmsford, New York: The Benjamin Company, Inc., 1987.

Quimby, George Irving. *Indian Life in the Upper Great Lakes, 11,000 B.C. to A.D. 1800.* Chicago: University of Chicago Press, 1960.

Ravinia: The Festival At Its Half Century. Ravinia Festival Association in conjunction with Rand McNally & Co., 1985.

Rickard, Ruth. *History of the College of Lake County 1969-1986.* Grayslake: The College of Lake County, 1987.

Rosen, Harry, and David Rosen. *But Not Next Door.* New York: Ivan Obolensky, Inc., 1962.

Schuberth, Christopher J. *A View of The Past: An Introduction to Illinois Geology.* Springfield: Illinois State Museum, 1986.

Schlesinger, Arthur M., Jr., ed. *The Almanac of American History.* New York: The Putnam Publishing Group, 1983.

Seymour, Ralph Fletcher. *Our Midwest.* Chicago: n.p., 1954.

Smith, Jesse Lowe. "Physical Geography of Lake County." In *A History of Lake County, Illinois,* edited by John J. Halsey. 1912.

Sprague, Paul E. *Final Report of the Historical Consultant on the Lake Forest, Ill. Ordinance Establishing a Residential Preservation District and Regulations Pertaining to It.* N.p., 1982.

Stern, Grace Mary. *With a Stern Eye.* Greater Lake County Press, n.d.

Tanner, Helen Hornbeck, ed. *Atlas of Great Lakes Indian History.* Norman, Oklahoma: The Newberry Library for University of Oklahoma Press, 1987.

Taylor, Jabez. *The Development of the City of Zion.* N.p., n.d.

Temple, Wayne C. *Indian Villages of the Illinois Country,* vol. 2, part 2. Springfield: Illinois State Museum, 1958.

Tennyson, Jon R. *$2500 and a Dream.* North Chicago: Fansteel, Inc., 1982.

Trychta, J.K., ed. *Lake Villa: A History of Our Town.* Lake Villa Public Library District, 1984.

Vliet, Elmer B. *Lake Bluff: The First 100 Years.* Lake Bluff: Elmer Vliet Historical Center, 1985.

Watters, Mary. *Illinois in the Second World War.* Springfield: Illinois State Historical Library, 1951.

Whitman, Alden. *A Stevenson Sampler 1945-1965.* New York: Harper & Row, 1965.

Wittelle, Marvyn. *Pioneer to Commuter.* Highland Park: The Rotary Club of Highland Park, 1958.

NEWSPAPERS
Antioch News
Chicago Tribune
Daily Herald
The News-Sun
Waukegan Daily Gazette Register
Waukegan Daily News
Waukegan Daily Sun
The Waukegan News-Sun
Waukegan Weekly Gazette

MANUSCRIPTS AND COLLECTIONS
Bradbury, Ray. File. Waukegan Public Library.

Dahringer, Homer. File. Lake County Museum.

Historical Map of Lake County, produced by Lake County Historical Society, 1954.

A History of Lake County Medicine 1835-1900 by David J. Kweder, M.D., and Adele Kweder. 1963. Waukegan Public Library Collection.

Illinois Land Records. Original Illinois Field Notes of Surveyors, 1800s. Newberry Library Collection.

Illinois War Department List of Dead and Missing, 1946. Waukegan Historical Society Collection.

School Histories, 1918. Lake County Museum.

Talcott, Jeduthan. Diary. Lake County Museum.

U.S. Navy Fact Sheets. Great Lakes Naval Training Center files.

Numerous other files from Lake County Museum and Waukegan Historical Society collections as well as libraries throughout the county and *The News-Sun* clip files.

INDEX